Museum
Cafés & Arts

Museum Cafés & Arts

by

SHARON O'CONNOR

INSPIRED RECIPES FROM FAVORITE MUSEUM CAFÉS
CHAMBER MUSIC BY THE ROSSETTI STRING QUARTET
ART FROM AMERICA'S GREAT MUSEUMS

MENUS AND MUSIC PRODUCTIONS, INC.
EMERYVILLE, CALIFORNIA

Printed in Korea

Library of Congress Catalog Card Number: 2002105192
O'Connor, Sharon
Menus and Music Volume XVII
Museum Cafés & Arts
    Inspired Recipes from Favorite Museum Cafés
    Chamber Music by the Rossetti String Quartet
    Art from America's Great Museums

Includes Index
1. Cookery 2. Entertaining
I. Title

ISBN 1-883914-34-5 (paperback with music compact disc)

Menus and Music Productions, Inc.
1462 66th Street
Emeryville, CA 94608
(510) 658-9100
www.menusandmusic.com

Design: Jennifer Barry Design, Sausalito
Layout Production: Kristen Wurz
Food photographer: Paul Moore
Food stylist: Amy Nathan
Prop stylist: Diane McGauley
Violin: Carlo Antonio Testori, 1741, Milan

Artwork page 1: MARY CASSATT *Afternoon Tea Party* 1890–1891,
National Gallery of Art
Artwork page 2: ORAZIO GENTILESCHI *The Lute Player* c. 1612/1620
National Gallery of Art
Artwork page 5: GUSTAVE CAILLEBOTTE *Fruit Displayed on a Stand* c. 1881–1882
Museum of Fine Arts, Boston
Artwork back cover: ORAZIO GENTILESCHI *The Lute Player* c. 1612/1620
National Gallery of Art; HENRI FANTIN-LATOUR *Still Life* 1866
National Gallery of Art

10 9 8 7 6 5 4 3

WASSILY KANDINSKY *Untitled Improvisation III* 1914 Los Angeles County Museum of Art

CONTENTS

INTRODUCTION

The arts not only give expression to the profound urgings of the human spirit; they also vali-
date our feeling in a world that deadens feeling. Now, more than ever, all people need to see
clearly, hear acutely, and feel sensitively through the arts. These skills are no longer just
desirable, they are essential if we are to survive together with civility and joy.

—Ernest L. Boyer

D uring the past year, it's been my great joy to visit art museums across America, cook all the delicious recipes in this book, record the Rossetti String quartet, and choose the art that is reproduced in this book! Intense and exhilarating, the year has had many magical moments.

One of those moments was an early Sunday afternoon at the Philadelphia Museum of Art. After a wondrous morning spent wandering through the galleries and period rooms, museum fatigue was beginning to set in. My husband and I sat down at a table in the Museum Restaurant, where we anticipated smoked salmon and delectable omelettes while listening to jazz played by a sensational vibes and bass duo. At that moment, the enjoyment of great art, brilliant music, and deli-cious food fused into an experience I'll long remember. We left the museum feeling replenished, both body and soul.

American art museums are one of our culture's few truly public spaces, and people are visiting them in droves! There are already more than 1,330 museums in the United States, and more than fifty major ones are currently in the process of being expanded and renovated. Working with celebrated architects and sometimes dealing with budgets in the hundreds of millions, museums have broad community support in cities across America.

In museums, we publicly interact with art and share an experience that reaf-firms civilized values and enlarges our understanding of other times and places. Great art reaches beyond the boundaries of reason and logic and speaks to the core of humanity in all of us. Standing in front of a masterpiece, we can experience a flash of consciousness that helps us to understand who we really are. When I saw Vermeer's *Young Woman with a Water Pitcher* (page 88) at The Metropolitan Museum, the painting distilled for me in a single gesture all women who have ever

BERTHE MORISOT *Soupière et Pomme (Tureen and Apple)* 1877 Denver Art Museum given sustenance and love to a family. In museums, we also experience the historical continuity of thousands of years of artistic creation, from Greek statues and Egyptian scarabs to Impressionist paintings and contemporary sculptures.

The sixteen museums included in this book are filled with every imaginable magnificence, from the astonishingly monumental to the exquisitely minimal. The art reproduced here includes prized works from each museum, as well as works that celebrate food, music, and festivity. They depict musicians, musical instruments, farmer's markets, fruits and vegetables, and meals enjoyed in the kitchen and out in the garden. I had a multitude of pieces to choose from that highlight the affinity between food, music, and art, but as wonderful as the reproductions are, they can't possibly do justice to the originals. I hope that someday you can make a pilgrimage to each of these museums to see the works in person.

Not only do all these museums shelter master paintings, drawings, and sculpture, they are also places to enjoy a concert or film, a beautiful garden, or a fine meal. Since no one can live on fine art alone, dining is now an inviting part of the experience at leading museums. I recommend each of the cafés in this book as a great place to eat, even if you don't have time to go through the galleries! Not that long ago, fine dining amid fine art, if available at all, was limited to staid members' dining rooms. But now museums are replacing their steam tables with fresh, exciting food cooked by talented chefs and served in stylish settings. Museum cafés are becoming destinations in themselves.

Museum café chefs have provided Menus and Music with some of their favorite recipes, and I've adapted them so that you can make the dishes at home. Some of my favorites are Butternut Squash Bisque, Salmon-Corn Cakes, Two-Bean and Roasted Beet Salad, Fig and Gorgonzola Tart, Spinach-and-Cheese Stuffed Chicken Breast with Marsala Sauce, Swordfish with Mushroom Ragout and Soft Parmesan Polenta, and Warm Bittersweet Chocolate Cakes. I hope the recipes will serve as a source of inspiration for some great home cooking. Go ahead and choose fresh herbs according to your own taste and vegetables and fruits according to seasonal availability—this kind of improvising makes cooking fun. And using your own creativity (and eating the delicious results!) is fundamentally satisfying.

For centuries, visual artists have played with musical themes and been inspired by music. I hope the glorious chamber music recorded here is an inspiration,

CAMILLE PISSARRO *The Artist's Garden at Eragny* 1898 The National Gallery

whether you are in the kitchen, at the table, or just in the mood to listen to music. In this recording, the members of the Rossetti String Quartet collaborate at their finest, and their ultra-sensitive playing is spellbinding.

Art, music, and delicious home-cooked meals enrich our lives, helping to make them multi-dimensional. Choosing to include these three great pleasures as part of daily life elevates our spirits. The human spirit will always make itself audible in music and visible in art, and we'll continue to turn to these ancient allied arts as surely as we'll always return to the table. I hope this volume gives you quiet moments of reflection and delicious moments of joy. To your health and happiness!

—*Sharon O'Connor*

MUSIC NOTES

Since Haydn began writing divertimentos in the mid-1700s for solo string instruments—two violins, viola, and cello—composers have never stopped composing for the string quartet. They have turned to it for the expression of some of their most intimate and ambitious music, and many, including Beethoven, Schubert, Bartók, Britten, and Shostakovich, wrote quartets during the last year of two of their lives. Just as many still lifes are regarded as "painter's paintings" because the artists revel in the challenges and pleasures of art, chamber music is what composers create for themselves and professional musicians play for fun. As modern life becomes more complex, clamorous, and depersonalized, chamber music has the power to touch us in a way that revitalizes our sensory world, helping to guarantee our sanity. Today there is more interest in string quartets than at any time since the time 240-odd years ago when they were established. During the 1970s there were only about thirty professional string quartets in North America, while today there are more than two hundred performing for devoted audiences.

When the members of the Rossetti String Quartet joined forces, they chose the nineteenth-century pre-Raphaelite painter Dante Gabriel Rossetti as their namesake. All four musicians felt an affinity with the painter's return to naturalism and lifelike color in a world that had grown complacent with the style of the times. Although the quartet members have diverse and distinguished backgrounds as soloists and chamber music players, they are unified by an abiding love for the string quartet literature and its presentation in a natural and very personal style. Their repertoire is based in the classic and romantic quartet tradition and extends into the contemporary literature. The Rossetti quartet concertizes worldwide and has performed at the Los Angeles County Museum and The J. Paul Getty Museum.

Here they have recorded a challenging and entertaining program of primarily second and third movements that span more than three centuries. These gorgeous inner movements were chosen to reflect the scope of the artwork presented in this book.

JOSEPH HAYDN (1732–1780)

Adagio, String Quartet, Op. 20 No. 5

Haydn began his career in the patronage system of the late Austrian Baroque and is one of the most celebrated composers of all time. Familiarly known as the father of the symphony and credited with establishing the substantial form of the string quartet, he composed more than one hundred symphonies and seventy-five string quartets. The third movement of Op. 20 No. 5 recorded here is one of six quartets written in 1772 when he was forty years old. The Adagio has a pastoral feeling, and the first violin's elaborate figurations above straightforward supporting harmonies are played with a subtle rhythmic freedom that foreshadows the rubato of Chopin.

WOLFGANG AMADEUS MOZART (1756–1791)

Andante, String Quartet, D Major, K. 575

"Before God and as an honest man I tell you that your son is the greatest composer known to me either in person or by name." These words by Joseph Haydn to Leopold Mozart are some of the most famous, and certainly most generous, statements ever made by one composer about another. Wolfgang Mozart excelled in every musical medium current in his time, especially in chamber music for strings, piano concertos, and opera. He composed twenty-seven string quartets, working brilliantly within the framework established by Haydn. The second movement recorded here was completed in 1789 and is one of three quartets Mozart composed for Friedrich Wilhelm II, the King of Prussia. Since the commissioner was an outstanding cellist, the cello is heard prominently throughout and often carries the melody in its higher register above the supportive second violin and viola.

LUDWIG VAN BEETHOVEN (1770–1827)

Andante scherzoso, String Quartet in C Minor, Op. 18 No. 4

Beethoven was the dominant musical figure of the nineteenth century and is probably the most admired composer in the history of Western music. He was devoted to chamber music composition from the age of fifteen, when he composed three piano quartets, to the days of his astounding late string quartets. In his early years, Beethoven worked on all types of chamber music but progressively concentrated on composing for string quartet. He expanded and modified the clear, concentrated structure that Haydn developed by adding broader lyricism and including repeated rhythmic patterns to create an effect of dynamism and power that intensified the styles of Haydn and Mozart. Count Waldstein prophetically wrote to Beethoven: "With the help of assiduous labor you shall inherit Mozart's spirit from Haydn's hands." Beethoven composed seventeen quartets and in his maturity produced quartets considered to be some of the greatest musical works ever created.

The Andante scherzoso quasi allegretto recorded here is the second movement of Op. 18 No. 4. This movement has a light fugal texture and subdued dynamics that offer a contrast to the quartet's other three movements, which are stormy and exciting.

MAURICE RAVEL (1875–1937)
Allegro moderato, String Quartet in F Major

One of the most original musicians of the early twentieth century, Ravel was generally regarded as France's leading composer after the death of his contemporary Debussy. Although not at the forefront of modernism, his advocacy of economy and his openness to jazz and bitonality was significant. Ravel's instrumental compositions for solo piano, chamber ensemble, and orchestra explore and develop new possibilities with a distinctly French sensibility and refinement. His fastidiously polished compositions also make important additions to the repertoire of French song and, with commissions from Diaghilev, to ballet. In 1903, he composed his first and only string quartet, a suave and melodious combination of classical form and modern harmony. The Rossetti's superb performance of the quartet's first movement is precisely beautiful.

CLAUDE DEBUSSY (1862–1918)
Andantino, doucement expressif, String Quartet in G Minor, Op. 10

Debussy is one of the greatest composers of French music and influenced almost all composers that followed him. His works are unusually independent of traditional form, harmony, and coloring, and his desire to free himself from tonality led him to the use of church modes and the whole-tone scale. Debussy's compositions brought a new rhythmic fluidity to classical composition, and his scoring was influenced by the Javanese gamelan, which he first heard in 1889 at the World Exhibition in Paris.

In 1893, while in his early thirties, Debussy completed his only string quartet. It follows traditional quartet structure, but its first performance shocked critics with its new harmonies and lack of traditionally developed themes. Although they thought it sounded like an "orgy of modulation" and seemed to attack the tradition of great French music, today the quartet is considered a high-water mark of modern chamber music. The third movement recorded here has a muted wealth of tonal colors, and the Rosetti's ultra-sensitive performance brings its delicate poetry to life.

SERGE RACHMANINOFF (1873–1943)

Romance from String Quartet in G Minor, Op. Posth.

Rachmaninoff was one of the finest pianists of his day and as a composer one of the last great representatives of Russian late Romanticism. The Romance heard here was written in 1889 and is one movement from a work that is sometimes titled Two Movements for String Quartet. The muted Andante espressivo has an absolutely gorgeous principal melody that is characteristic of Rachmaninoff's lyricism. The Romance is followed by a quick Scherzo, and the manuscript indicates that these movements were planned as the middle pair of a complete quartet. Rachmaninoff arranged the work for orchestra in 1890, and it received a performance the following year. The Rossetti's performance of this gorgeous movement is played as one long sentence.

ALEXANDER BORODIN (1833–1887)

Nocturne from String Quartet in D Major

Borodin was a distinguished research chemist and professor in St. Petersburg as well as one of Russia's greatest composers and an amateur cellist. He finished his second string quartet in 1885 and dedicated it to his wife. His friend and biographer, Serge Dianin, suggests that "the *Nocturne* is simply a love scene." This is one of the most famous movements in all chamber music. It is included as "And This is My Beloved" in *Kismet*, a musical derived from Borodin's music.

ANTONIN DVOŘÁK (1841–1904)

Dumka. Andante con moto from String Quartet Op. 51

One of the great nationalist Czech composers of the nineteenth century, Dvořák was a viola player himself, and string quartet composition always remained central to his work. His Op. 51 was commissioned by the Florentine Quartet, who requested a work in "Slavonic" style. The second movement heard here opens with a melancholy theme in G minor, which alternates with a vivace section in G major that incorporates a quick Bohemian dance with shifting accents.

HEITOR VILLA-LOBOS (1887–1959) *Third Movement from String Quartet, No. 5*
The most significant composer of twentieth-century Brazilian music, Villa Lobos's compositions blend European techniques and his reinterpretations of national music. The works produced by this self-taught composer include more than two thousand pieces, including seventeen string quartets. His compositions have tremendous range, from classical to experimental and folkloristic. As a youth, he studied cello, but he loved Rio de Janeiro's popular idioms, which had lasting influence in his compositions. Villa Lobos made an exhaustive four-year study of folk songs, collecting them from all over Brazil. He composed his fifth string quartet in 1931 and subtitled it "Quarteto popular." In the third movement recorded here, we hear his reshaping of Brazilian folk melodies and harmonies.

GEORGE GERSHWIN (1898–1937) *Lullaby*
George Gershwin began his musical career as a pianist and song plugger in Tin Pan Alley. Here he learned what was involved in producing hit tunes, and his piano technique improved immensely from playing eight or ten hours a day. The job also gave him an opportunity to improvise at the piano, experimenting with new runs, chords, and modulations. During these early years, he studied composition with Edward Kilenyi and Rubin Goldmark, among others. The charming Lullaby recorded here was probably composed when he was twenty-one and studying with one of those men. Gershwin died in his prime at the age of thirty-eight, but he left us with hundreds of his immensely popular songs, as well as *Rhapsody in Blue*, *Porgy and Bess*, and *An American in Paris*.

ENRIQUE FRANCINI (1916–1978) *"La vi llegar"*
A brilliant Argentinian violinist, orchestra leader, and composer, Francini's career was centered in Buenos Aires. During the early 1940s, he performed in the all-star dance orchestra of Miguel Caló, one of the city's most popular. He started his own tango orchestra in 1955 and made a recording for RCA-Victor. The tango, the most popular Argentinian urban dance of the twentieth century, remains one of the most expressive and nationalistic symbols of Argentine character. Internationally fashionable, it became popular in Parisian salons, English ballrooms, and American restaurants. Francini was the violinist of an octet founded by Astor Piazzolla, and during the 1960s he was first violinist at the Teatro Colón, the fabled Buenos Aires opera house.

VALENTIN DE BOULOGNE *A Musical Party* c. 1626 Los Angeles County Museum of Art

Often some of the finest works in a museum are not by the most famous artists. One of LACMA's most important recent acquisitions is a painting of a musical party by Valentin de Boulogne. I just knew of him as a respected follower of Caravaggio, but I was ravished by his use of color. Not only the bright orange of the man's sleeve, but the subtle flesh tones, with the boy's five o'clock shadow and the high cheekbone of the gypsy girl. Scholars differ as to the theme of this picture, but it seems to me, and I'll fight you on this one, it seems to me that this is about the power of music. They all come from different walks of society. The boy in his rather scruffy get up, the gypsy girl who was probably a prostitute, the respectable old man with his well-combed beard, the soldier with his sword. Nothing brings them together except music, and they're lusting it. I used to think the girl was yearning towards the boy. But I've recently seen exactly that expression on the face of an accompanist trying to keep in tone and in tune with another player. They're not aware of each other as people, they're just aware of the music. And the man at the back, well armored, drinking, he's the one who's out of the magic circle because he finds his pleasure in wine. There's poignancy for me in this picture because at home in the trailer I live in silence. Now I want that, I choose it, I wouldn't have it different, but this makes me realize how much I'm missing.

—Sister Wendy Beckett, excerpt from the public television series
Sister Wendy's American Collection. Quoted with permission from WGBH.

PIERRE-AUGUSTE RENOIR *Lunch at the Restaurant Fournaise (The Rowers' Lunch)* 1875

THE ART INSTITUTE OF CHICAGO
CHICAGO, ILLINOIS

The Art Institute of Chicago is more than a museum, it's a vital and evolving tabernacle of time travel, overflowing with stories and secrets in every single work of art. It's a continually changing discovery zone, enjoyed by millions of people a year, and a uniquely American, uniquely Midwestern cultural institution.

—Brian Dennehy, Actor and narrator of
"Treasures of the Art Institute," WTTW/Chicago

One of the premier art institutions in the world, the Art Institute of Chicago houses more than 300,000 works of art within its ten curatorial departments. Among its great treasures are the legendary masterpieces *American Gothic* by Grant Wood, *Nighthawks* (page 22) by Edward Hopper, *A Sunday on La Grand Jatte—1884* by George Seurat, *Paris Street; Rainy Day* by Gustave Caillebotte, and thirty-three paintings by Claude Monet.

In 1866, a small group of artists founded the Chicago Academy of Design. After the Great Chicago Fire in 1871, the Academy was reorganized under the name Chicago Academy of Fine Art. The young institution's mission was to "found, build, maintain, and operate museums of fine arts, schools, and libraries of art... conducive to the artistic development of the community." In 1882, the Academy formally changed its name to The Art Institute of Chicago. The museum moved into a new Beaux-Arts building following the World's Fair of 1893, and although this monumental structure has been expanded and renovated many times during the last century, it remains the Art Institute's home to this day. In 2000, the Art Institute announced plans for a new building and gardens to be designed by award-winning Italian architect Renzo Piano. His dramatic twenty-first-century building, which will be located within the Grant Park complex and provide a strong link to the existing Art Institute, is expected to be completed in 2007.

The Art Institute offers visitors a trip through the great cultures of the world, and each year mounts more than 25 exhibitions from its vast permanent collections. The internationally-renowned collection of French Impressionist and Post-Impressionist paintings are visitor favorites, as are the Berman Galleries of Surrealist Art, which includes the largest grouping of Joseph Cornell boxes and collages in the world. Other highlights are Marc Chagall's magnificent stained glass windows commissioned to commemorate Chicago's late Mayor Richard J. Daley, a delightful collection of paperweights, and the sixty-eight Thorne Miniature Rooms—small-scale recreations of rooms in American and European homes from the seventeenth century to the 1930s. Families enjoy the museum's lively Kraft Education Center, with interactive exhibitions for young people; artists' demonstrations; and a Family Reading Room for sharing books and relaxing between gallery visits. An annual series of chamber music is performed by members of the Chicago Symphony Orchestra and introduced by slide lectures on topics related to the music and followed by gallery walks. This is but one of many programs involving musicians, actors, dancers, and writers that bring together the performing and visual arts. The School of the Art Institute, one of the few principal colleges of art and design affiliated with a major museum in the United States, has two galleries open to the public, as well as the Gene Siskel Film Center.

Dining options at the Art Institute include the Court Cafeteria for casual meals and snacks; The Garden Restaurant, a lovely outdoor café open June through September; and The Restaurant on the Park, with acclaimed cuisine and expansive views of Grant Park. The Restaurant is bright and airy and its elegant design integrates architectural fragments from three Chicago buildings by the architect Louis Sullivan. Outside in the garden but visible from the dining room, is the Stock Exchange arch, and there is a reconstruction of the Adler and Sullivan trading room of the Chicago Stock Exchange that is visible from the dining room foyer. The following recipes were created by executive chef Yves Petitcolas and pastry chef Peter Rios of The Restaurant on the Park.

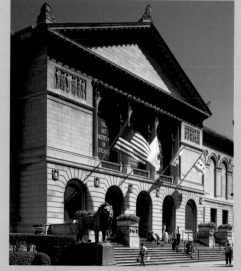

WINSLOW HOMER *For to Be a Farmer's Boy (old English song)* 1887

EDWARD HOPPER *Nighthawks* 1942

CRAB CAKES WITH
CILANTRO-GINGER RÉMOULADE

The delicate flavor of crab is delicious with this refreshing rémoulade. If crabmeat is unavailable, the dish can be prepared with flaked poached salmon or halibut instead.

CRAB CAKES

8 ounces (250 g) fresh lump crabmeat, picked over for shell

2 roasted garlic cloves (see Basics)

$1/4$ cup ($1/2$ oz/15 g) fresh bread crumbs

$1/4$ bunch chives, minced

Leaves from $1/4$ bunch cilantro, minced

Grated zest and juice of $1/2$ lemon

$1/2$ small red onion, finely chopped

$1/3$ cup (3 oz/90 g) mayonnaise

$1/4$ teaspoon ground coriander

Salt, paprika, and cayenne pepper to taste

CILANTRO-GINGER RÉMOULADE

Leaves from 1 small bunch cilantro

1 tablespoon mined peeled fresh ginger

$1/3$ cup (3 oz/90 g) mayonnaise or $1/3$ cup (3 fl oz/80 ml) olive oil

1 tablespoon Dijon mustard

7 cornichons

1 tablespoon capers

Grated zest and juice of $1/2$ lemon

Salt, paprika, and cayenne pepper to taste

(continued)

Vinaigrette

2 tablespoons fresh lemon juice
6 tablespoons (3 fl oz/90 ml) extra-virgin olive oil
Salt and freshly ground pepper to taste

2 tablespoons olive oil
4 handfuls mixed baby salad greens

■ To make the crab cakes: In a large bowl, gently stir all the ingredients together. Shape the mixture into 6 patties; they will barely hold together. Transfer to a platter lined with waxed paper, cover with plastic wrap, and refrigerate for 1 hour.
■ In a blender or food processor, combine all the rémoulade ingredients and purée. Cover and refrigerate until chilled.
■ In a medium bowl, whisk all the vinaigrette ingredients together. Add the salad greens to the vinaigrette and toss until well mixed.
■ In a large frying pan over medium-high heat, heat the olive oil until almost smoking. Sauté the crab cakes for 2 to 3 minutes on each side, or until golden brown.
■ To serve, arrange a bed of salad on each of 6 plates. Place a crab cake on top and dollop with the rémoulade. *Makes 6 servings*

The Art Institute of Chicago

JAN STEEN *The Family Concert* 1666

PORK LOIN CHOPS
WITH APPLE-TARRAGON CHUTNEY

The lively sweet-tart chutney and cider glaze enhance the pork's delicate flavor. This is delicious served with mashed Yukon Gold potatoes and roasted shallots.

CIDER GLAZE

4 cups (32 fl oz/1 l) apple juice

2 cardamom pods

1 cinnamon stick

1/4 cup (1/3 oz/10 g) coriander seeds

1 teaspoon cumin seeds

1 teaspoon fennel seeds

1/3 cup (3 fl oz/90 ml) cider vinegar

APPLE-TARRAGON CHUTNEY

1/2 cup (4 fl oz/125 ml) cider glaze, above

2 Granny Smith apples, peeled, cored, and diced

Leaves from 1/4 bunch fresh tarragon, minced

2 tablespoons olive oil

4 boneless loin pork chops, each about 3/4 inch (2 cm) thick

Salt and freshly ground pepper to taste

■ In a medium saucepan, combine all the cider glaze ingredients. Bring to a boil and cook to reduce to about 1 cup. Remove from heat and strain through a fine-mesh sieve into a bowl.

■ To make the chutney: Return the cider glaze to the same saucepan (see above). Stir in the apples, bring to a boil over high heat, and cook for 2 minutes. Remove from heat and stir in the tarragon.

■ Preheat the oven to 350°F (180°C). Season the pork chops with salt and pepper on both sides. In a large ovenproof frying pan over medium-high heat, heat the olive oil until it shimmers. Add the pork chops, reduce heat to medium, and cook for 2 to 3 minutes on each side, or until lightly browned. Transfer the chops to a baking dish and bake in the preheated oven until an instant-read thermometer inserted in the center of a chop registers 150°F (65°C). Serve the pork drizzled with cider glaze, with a dollop of chutney alongside. *Makes 4 servings*

COCONUT CREAM AND PINEAPPLE-LIME TART

Tropical flavors combine in this luscious layered tart.

TART DOUGH

$^1/_2$ cup (4 oz/125 g) cold unsalted
  butter, cut into pieces

$^1/_2$ cup (4 oz/125 g) sugar

2 egg yolks

1 cup (5 oz/155 g) all-purpose flour

COCONUT DAQUOISE

3 egg whites

$^1/_2$ cup (4 oz/125 g) sugar

$^2/_3$ cup (3 oz/90 g) ground almonds

$^1/_2$ cup (2 oz/60 g) crumbled coconut
  macaroons (see Basics)

COCONUT CREAM

2 teaspoons unflavored gelatin

$^1/_4$ cup (2 fl oz/60 ml) water

1 cup (8 fl oz/250 ml) heavy cream

2 egg yolks

$^1/_2$ cup (4 oz/125 g) sugar

3 tablespoons coconut cream

PINEAPPLE-LIME TOPPING

$^1/_2$ fresh pineapple, peeled, cored, and
  finely diced

Grated zest and juice of 1 lime

Mango Coulis (page 98) for serving

Crème Anglaise (see Basics) for
  serving

■ To make the tart dough: In a food processor, combine the butter and sugar and
process to blend. With the machine running, add the egg yolks one at a time.
Add the flour and process just until the dough forms a ball, add water if necessary.
Transfer the dough to a lightly floured work surface. Flatten the dough into a disk,
cover with plastic wrap, and refrigerate for 1 hour.

■ Preheat the oven to 375°F (190°C). On a lightly floured surface, roll the
dough out to a round 10 inches (25 cm) in diameter. Fit the dough into a 9-inch
(23-cm) tart pan. Trim the edges and prick the bottom with a fork. Line the
shell with aluminum foil and fill with dried beans or pastry weights. Bake in the
preheated oven for 20 minutes, or until set. Remove the beans or weights and
aluminum foil. Transfer the pan to a wire rack and let cool.

■ To make the dacquoise: Preheat the oven to 350°F (180°C). In a medium
bowl, beat the egg whites until soft peaks form. Beat in $^1/_4$ cup (2 oz/60 g) of the

sugar. Fold in the almonds, macaroons, and remaining $^1/4$ cup (2 oz/60 g) sugar. Spoon the dacquoise into the prebaked tart shell. Bake in the preheated oven for 10 minutes, or until the top is browned. Remove from the oven and let cool completely.

■ To make the coconut cream: Sprinkle the gelatin over the cold water, and without stirring, let it absorb the water for about 2 minutes. In a medium, heavy saucepan, whisk the cream, egg yolks, and sugar together until blended. Cook over low heat, stirring constantly, until barely warm. Remove from heat and stir in the gelatin and coconut cream. Pour the mixture into a bowl and set it in a bowl of ice cubes. Whisk constantly until cooled to room temperature. Spoon over the dacquoise into the tart shell. Cover and refrigerate for 2 hours, or until set.

■ Meanwhile, stir all the topping ingredients together in a medium bowl. Set aside for at least 30 minutes. Drain well. Spoon over the chilled tart.

■ To serve, cut the tart into 8 wedges. Decorate each of 8 plates with mango coulis and crème anglaise. Arrange a slice of tart in the center of each plate and serve. *Makes 8 servings*

THE ART INSTITUTE OF CHICAGO

NICOLAS POUSSIN *The Holy Family on the Steps* 1648

THE CLEVELAND MUSEUM OF ART
CLEVELAND, OHIO

I think the Cleveland Museum of Art speaks for itself. You have to come down. No amount of talking or proselytizing is going to do what a visit is going to do . . . as we walk in this museum we just stumble upon masterpiece after masterpiece.

—Wynton Marsalis

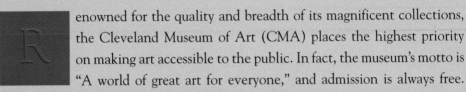enowned for the quality and breadth of its magnificent collections, the Cleveland Museum of Art (CMA) places the highest priority on making art accessible to the public. In fact, the museum's motto is "A world of great art for everyone," and admission is always free. Founded in 1916, the museum's marble-clad Beaux-Arts building overlooks the Fine Arts Garden and is located on fifteen acres of land in the famed University Circle area, also home to the Cleveland Music School Settlement, Case Western University, and the Cleveland Botanical Garden. An expansion of the museum by architect Rafael Viñoly is planned for the near future. Many people choose to visit the museum during one of its annual public festivals, such as the Family Festival of African Drum and Dance, the Chalk Festival, or the Parade the Circle Celebration, an international Carnival-inspired event that draws thousands each June.

The Cleveland museum's permanent collection spans more than five thousand years and includes Old Masters paintings by Caravaggio, Hals, and Rubens, and Impressionist masterpieces by Monet, Degas, and Renoir. Cleveland's comprehensive Asian and medieval European art collections are particularly notable, and its holdings in pre-Columbian objects are among the finest in North America. The Armor Court is especially popular, as is treasures of royal families, with its jewel-encrusted Fabergé eggs and a bed that once belonged to Marie Antoinette. Visitors can learn more about the permanent collections by taking the Sight & Sound CD audio tour, with lively descriptions and background information about more than three hundred works of art.

The CMA is a major center for music and film in northeast Ohio. The VIVA! Festival of Performing Arts is a popular venue for world music, and the museum's performing arts calendar includes the Gala Music Series of chamber music concerts, the Jazz on the Circle series, and special exhibition-related programs. The museum's department of Education and Public Programs reaches out to the Cleveland community with a teacher resource center; interactive video-conference classes for Ohio schools; and Art to Go, a program that allows volunteers to bring works of art into classrooms for thematic lessons.

During the summer months, thousands of people attend the museum's Summer Evenings in the Courtyard events, which feature jazz concerts and outdoor dining every Wednesday and Friday evening. The self-service Still Lifes Café offers housemade soups, sandwiches, and entrées to hungry museum visitors, and on Sundays there is a sumptuous brunch in The Oasis and Fountain Rooms, which overlook the outdoor sculpture and trees of the museum's lovely courtyard. The seasonal menus at the Still Lifes Café and The Oasis restaurant are designed to complement current exhibitions.

The Armor Court, The Cleveland Museum of Art

JUSTE-AURÈLE MEISSONIER *Tureen* 1735–1740

LOBSTER AND CORN RAVIOLI

Prepare the broth the evening before you plan to serve the ravioli. Salmon may be substituted for the lobster. Delicious with a glass of chilled Chardonnay.

10 ears fresh corn, shucked

BROTH
10 fresh corn cobs, above
2 bay leaves
Salt and freshly ground pepper to taste

FILLING
2 tablespoons unsalted butter
1 onion, finely chopped

Corn kernels cut from 10 ears fresh corn, above
6 ounces (185 g) cooked lobster meat, diced
Salt and freshly ground pepper to taste

Twelve 3-inch (7.5-cm) wonton skins
1 egg, beaten
Finely shredded fresh basil for garnish

■ Using a large sharp knife, cut the corn kernels from each ear of corn. Reserve both the kernels and the cobs.

■ To make the broth: In a large pot, combine the reserved corn cobs and the bay leaf. Add water to just cover. Bring to a boil over high heat, reduce heat to low, and simmer for 2 hours. Strain the broth through a fine-mesh sieve into a saucepan. Cook over high heat to reduce it by half. Season with salt and pepper. Remove from heat, let cool, and refrigerate.

■ To make the filling: In a large frying pan, melt the butter over medium heat and sauté the onion for 3 minutes, or until translucent. Add the reserved corn kernels and sauté for 5 minutes, or until tender. Transfer to a blender or food processor and purée. Stir in the lobster meat and season with salt and pepper.

■ Place 1 tablespoon filling in the center of each wonton skin. Brush the 2 adjoining edges with the beaten egg and fold the skin in half to form a triangle. Press the edges firmly to seal. Carefully add the ravioli to a large pot of salted, slowly boiling water and cook for 3 to 4 minutes, or until they float to the top. Using a wire-mesh skimmer, carefully transfer them to a bowl.

■ To serve, arrange 3 ravioli in the bottom of each of 4 shallow soup bowls, ladle in the broth, and garnish with the basil. *Makes 4 servings*

SAUTÉED DUCK BREASTS WITH SWISS CHARD AND GINGER-BRAISED CELERY

Richly flavorful duck meat, paired with braised chard and a citrus vinaigrette, makes a superb, balanced dish.

VINAIGRETTE
3 tablespoons fresh orange juice
1 teaspoon fresh lemon juice
1/4 cup (2 fl oz/60 ml) olive oil
Salt and freshly ground pepper to taste
1 green onion, white part only, finely
    chopped
1 orange, peeled and segmented
    (see Basics)

2 tablespoons unsalted butter
2 tablespoons minced peeled fresh
    ginger
4 celery stalks, sliced diagonally
1 cup (8 fl oz/250 ml) chicken stock
    (see Basics) or canned low-salt
    chicken broth
1 bunch Swiss chard, stemmed and
    chopped
4 boneless duck breast halves, skin on
1 tablespoon minced mixed fresh
    herbs, such as thyme, rosemary,
    and sage

■ To make the vinaigrette: In a small bowl, whisk together the orange juice, lemon juice, olive oil, salt, and pepper together. Stir in the green onion and orange segments.

■ In a large frying pan, melt the butter over medium heat and sauté the ginger and celery for 2 minutes. Add the stock or broth and simmer for 5 minutes. Stir in the Swiss chard and cook for 3 to 4 minutes, or until tender.

■ Using a sharp knife, score a crisscross pattern in the skin of the duck breasts and sprinkle with salt and pepper. In a large frying pan over low heat, cook the duck breasts, skin side down, for 7 to 8 minutes, or until crisp and golden brown on the bottom. Pour off the fat. Turn the breasts over and cook for 3 to 4 minutes on the second side for medium rare. Transfer the duck to a cutting board, skin side up, and cut into thin diagonal slices.

■ Arrange a mound of celery and Swiss chard in the center of each of 4 plates. Fan the duck slices on top and spoon the vinaigrette over. Garnish with herbs and serve immediately. *Makes 4 servings*

COUSCOUS CUSTARD
WITH RAISIN AND BERRY COMPOTE

Soothing custard served with a fruity compote.

CUSTARD
1 cup (8 fl oz/250 ml) water
1 envelope unflavored gelatin
$^1/_2$ cup (4 oz/60 g) couscous
1 cup (8 fl oz/125 ml) heavy cream
  or half-and-half
$^1/_2$ cup (4 fl oz/125 ml) milk
$^1/_2$ cup (4 oz/125 g) sugar
1 vanilla bean, split lengthwise, or
  1 teaspoon vanilla extract

COMPOTE
$^1/_2$ cup (4 fl oz/125 ml) sugar syrup
  (see Basics)
$^3/_4$ cup (4 oz/125 g) raisins

2 cups (8 oz/250 g) fresh raspberries,
  blackberries, or halved hulled
  strawberries

Whipped cream for garnish (optional)
4 sprigs fresh mint for garnish
  (optional)

■ To make the custard: Pour $^1/_4$ cup (2 fl oz/60 ml) water into a cup. Sprinkle the gelatin over the water and let it sit for about 2 minutes.

■ In a small saucepan, bring the remaining $^3/_4$ cup (6 fl oz/185 ml) water to a boil over high heat and stir in the couscous. Bring to a boil, then reduce heat to low. Cover and simmer for 1 minute. Remove from heat and let stand for 5 minutes. Fluff the couscous with a fork.

■ In a medium saucepan, combine the cream or half-and-half, milk, sugar, and vanilla bean, if using. Slowly bring to a boil over low heat. Remove from heat and set aside for 5 minutes to let the vanilla flavor infuse the milk. Remove the vanilla bean. Stir in the gelatin mixture, couscous, and vanilla extract, if using. Lightly oil four 3-inch (7-cm) ramekins. Spoon the custard into the molds and refrigerate for 1 hour, or until set.

■ In a medium saucepan, combine all the compote ingredients. Simmer for 10 minutes. Remove from heat.

■ Unmold a custard onto each of 4 plates and spoon a little of the compote over. Garnish with whipped cream and a sprig of mint, if desired. *Makes 4 servings*

PIETER DE HOOCH *Portrait of a Family Playing Music* 1663

EDOUARD MANET *Vase of White Lilacs and Roses* 1883

DALLAS MUSEUM OF ART
DALLAS, TEXAS

Our museum is going to be one hundred in 2003 and that is very exciting for a city as young as Dallas. We have been very fortunate in the past to have patrons that bought art early, and because of them, we have an outstanding collection of paintings by Monet and Mondrian, and we are developing a collection of Gerhard Richter's works. Our museum's various collections—from African, ancient American, Indonesian, American decorative, to contemporary art—appeal to people from all walks of life, and the museum is known for its community education programs. Our museum is located in the Arts District, near Meyerson Symphony Center and adjoining the Nasher Sculpture Center. —Roger Horchow

T he permanent collections of the Dallas Museum of Art (DMA) are comprehensive and well displayed in an elegant, expansive setting. Highlights include the Southwest's most significant holdings in African art; masterpieces by American painters such as Jackson Pollock, Mark Rothko, Jasper Johns, and Andy Warhol; and impressive holdings in European art of the early twentieth century, including early and late works by Piet Mondrian. Paintings by Renoir, Van Gogh, Pissarro, Cézanne and other Impressionist and Post-Impressionist artists are displayed in galleries that evoke a villa on the French Riviera—as stipulated by the donors. Recently, the DMA added seminal Cubist works by Pablo Picasso, Georges Braque, and Juan Gris, and there is a superb collection of paintings of the Hudson River School. The art of the Americas is represented with Pre-Columbian treasures, Spanish Colonial art, and a collection of paintings, sculpture, and decorative arts by artists such as Thomas Cole, John Singer Sargent, Edward Hopper, and Georgia O'Keeffe. The Dallas museum's large sculpture garden is restful and inviting, with cascading waterfalls, reflecting pools, and nineteenth- and twentieth-century art.

The museum was established in 1903 as the Dallas Art Association and moved in 1936 to its first permanent home at the Texas State Fair Grounds. In the 1960s, the DMA merged with the Dallas Museum of Contemporary Art. In 1983, the museum moved downtown into an impressive limestone building designed by architect Edward Larrabee Barnes when Dallas created the Arts District.

On Thursday evenings, DMA visitors can enjoy live jazz, lectures, and films that cover a broad spectrum of interests. The Gateway Gallery offers art activities

MENU
SEVENTEEN SEVENTEEN RESTAURANT

■

*Tecate Shrimp and
Queso Fresco in Poblano Crepes
with Tomatillo Salsa*

*Molasses-Rubbed Smoked Pork
Tenderloin with
Saffron Grits and
Grilled-Pineapple Chutney*

*Gooey Dark and
White Chocolate Cakes
with Raspberry Sauce*

for children and their families, including a three-dimensional version of Edward Hick's *Peaceable Kingdom* and an African hut with a Senufo drum. In addition, Family Days provide opportunities for enjoying music, storytelling, art projects, and more. One of the most innovative outreach programs at the museum is its literary series, Arts & Letters Live. There are presentations by distinguished writers, an off-site literary café, and Texas Bound events, which feature actors reading short stories by Texas writers.

Museum-goers who want to take a break can visit the Atrium Café and enjoy soups, salads, and sandwiches in a casual setting. The museum's acclaimed Seventeen Seventeen restaurant is a destination for fine dining. Contemporary American cuisine, with Asian and Southwestern influences, is artfully presented here in a polished gallery-like setting.

Double-chamber palm wine vessel c. 1900–1930
Africa, Democratic Republic of the Congo, Uele subregion, Mangbetu people

PAUL GAUGUIN *Under the Pandanus (I Raro te Oviri)* 1891

TECATE SHRIMP AND QUESO FRESCO IN POBLANO CREPES WITH TOMATILLO SALSA

If you can't find queso fresco, a fresh Mexican cheese, substitute mozzarella. Serve these crepes as a first course or as a light supper with a crisp green salad.

POBLANO CREPE BATTER

1 poblano chili or small green bell pepper, roasted, peeled, and finely diced (see Basics)

2 eggs, beaten

1 cup (8 fl oz/250 ml) milk

$1/2$ cup ($2^1/2$ oz/75 g) all-purpose flour

2 tablespoons brown butter (see Basics)

1 teaspoon salt

Corn or canola oil for brushing, plus oil for deep-frying and 2 tablespoons

2 ears fresh corn, shucked

$1/2$ cup ($2^1/2$ oz/75 g) cornmeal

$1/2$ cup ($2^1/2$ oz/75 g) all-purpose flour

Salt and freshly ground pepper to taste

1 cup (8 fl oz/250 ml) beer, preferably Tecate

8 ounces (250 g) large shrimp, shelled, deveined, and cut in half crosswise

$1^1/2$ cups (8 oz/250 g) crumbled queso fresco or shredded mozzarella cheese

Tomatillo Salsa for serving (recipe follows)

■ In a medium bowl, combine all the crepe batter ingredients and whisk until smooth. Cover and refrigerate to at least 1 hour or up to 2 days.

■ Heat an 8-inch (20-cm) nonstick or seasoned crepe batter pan over medium heat until a drop of water flicked on the surface jumps around. Brush the pan with oil. Pour in a scant $1/4$ cup (2 fl oz/60 ml) of the batter. Immediately tilt the pan to spread evenly. Cook until the edge of the crepe is dry, about 1 minute. Loosen with a plastic spatula or your fingers and flip it over. Cook for 30 seconds to 1 minute. Transfer the crepe to a plate. Repeat, stacking the 8 crepes.

■ Preheat the oven to 450°F (230°C). Wrap the ears of corn tightly in aluminum foil and place in a shallow baking dish. Bake in the preheated oven for 20 minutes. Remove from the oven and let cool. Use a sharp knife to cut off the kernels.

■ In a medium bowl, combine the cornmeal, flour, salt, and pepper. Whisk in the beer until smooth. Coat each shrimp with the batter.

(continued)

- In a Dutch oven or large, heavy pot, heat 1 inch (2.5 cm) oil over medium-high heat to 365°F (185°C), or until almost smoking. Working in batches, carefully add the shrimp to the hot oil and deep-fry for about 3 minutes, or until golden brown. Using a slotted spoon, transfer to paper towels to drain.
- In a large frying pan over medium-high heat, heat the 2 tablespoons oil and sauté the corn kernels and cheese until the cheese melts. Stir in the shrimp. Spoon one-eighth of the filling in a line across the center of each crepe. Fold each crepe in half. Arrange 1 or 2 crepes on each plate and serve immediately, with the tomatillo salsa. *Makes 8 first-course or 4 main-course servings*

TOMATILLO SALSA

6 tomatillos*, husked, rinsed, and
halved
2 cups (16 fl oz/500 ml) chicken stock
(see Basics), canned low-salt
chicken broth, or water

1 jalapeno chili, seeded and minced
1 onion, quartered
Salt to taste

- In a medium saucepan, combine all the ingredients and bring to a boil over high heat. Cook for 5 minutes. Reduce heat to low and simmer for 20 to 30 minutes, or until the sauce has thickened. Remove from heat, transfer to a blender or food processor, and coarsely purée. Serve warm or at room temperature.

* Tomatillos resemble small green tomatoes with a paper-thin husk. They are available in the produce section of many supermarkets and in Latino markets.

MOLASSES-RUBBED SMOKED PORK TENDERLOIN WITH SAFFRON GRITS AND GRILLED-PINEAPPLE CHUTNEY

Tender pork with a bright relish, served on a bed of richly flavored grits. The pork may be smoked in a charcoal grill or in a wok. The chutney also makes a great topping for grilled poultry and fish.

1^1/$_2$ pounds (24 oz/750 g) pork
   tenderloin
^{1}/$_4$ cup (2^1/$_2$ oz/75 g) molasses
Salt and freshly ground pepper to taste
2 cups apple wood chips

Grilled-Pineapple Chutney
4 slices fresh pineapple, each ^{1}/$_2$ inch
   (12 mm) thick, peeled and cored
2 tablespoons sugar

^{1}/$_4$ cup (2 fl oz/60 ml) white wine
   vinegar
4 fresh chives, chopped
2 tablespoons finely diced red bell
   pepper
Salt to taste

Canola oil for filming pan (optional)
Saffron Grits (recipe follows)

■ Rub the pork with the molasses and sprinkle with salt and pepper. Set aside to marinate for 1 hour.

■ Light a fire in a charcoal grill if using to smoke the pork or preheat a broiler if using a wok to smoke the pork. Soak the apple wood chips in water at least 30 minutes

■ To make the pineapple chutney: Grill or broil the pineapple slices for 2 to 3 minutes on each side, or until lightly charred. Let cool and dice; set aside.

■ In a small saucepan over medium-low heat, combine the sugar and vinegar. Cook over medium-low heat until syrupy, about 5 minutes. Remove from heat and stir in the pineapple, chives, bell pepper, and salt.

■ Drain the wood chips and sprinkle over the coals. Open all the vents of the charcoal grill. Place the pork on the grill, cover, and cook the pork, turning several times, for about 30 minutes, or until an instant-read thermometer inserted into the thickest part of the pork registers 160°F (70°C).

(continued)

DALLAS MUSEUM OF ART

- Alternatively, line a wok with two 24-by-18-inch (60-by-45-cm) pieces of heavy-duty aluminum foil, allowing the excess foil to hang over the sides. Place the pork tenderloin on a round wire rack that will just fit inside the wok; set aside. Drain the chips and spread them out in the wok. Cover the wok with a lid and heat over high heat until smoke seeps out, 10 to 15 minutes. Working quickly, uncover the wok and place the rack with the pork in the wok. Cover with the lid and seal with the over-hanging foil. Remove from heat and set aside; do not disturb for 30 minutes.
- Meanwhile, preheat the oven to 350°F (180°C). Remove the pork from the wok. In a large oiled frying pan over medium-high heat, sear the pork until browned on all sides. Roast in the preheated oven until an instant-read thermometer inserted into the thickest part of the pork registers 160°F (70°C).
- To serve, cut the pork into thin slices. Place a scoop of grits in the center of each of 4 plates. Arrange slices of pork on top and garnish with pineapple chutney; serve at once. *Makes 4 servings*

SAFFRON GRITS

2 tablespoons canola oil
2 tablespoons minced shallots
2 tablespoons minced garlic
1 cup (6 oz/185 g) instant grits
2 tomatoes, diced

3 to 4 cups (24 to 32 fl oz/750 ml to 1 l) chicken stock (see Basics) or canned low-salt chicken broth
Pinch of saffron threads
3 tablespoons unsalted butter
1/4 cup (1 oz/30 g) grated Parmesan cheese (optional)
Salt and freshly ground pepper to taste

- In a medium saucepan over medium heat, heat the canola oil and sauté the shallots and garlic for 2 minutes, or until the shallots are translucent. Add the tomatoes, salt, and pepper and cook for 5 minutes, or until the tomatoes are soft. Stir in the stock or broth and saffron; raise heat to high and bring to a boil. Gradually stir in the grits and cook for 5 to 6 minutes, or until thickened. If the grits are too thick, add more stock or broth. Stir in the butter, Parmesan, salt, and pepper. Serve hot.

GOOEY DARK AND WHITE CHOCOLATE CAKES WITH RASPBERRY SAUCE

These delightful little cakes have molten dark chocolate interiors.

DARK CHOCOLATE BATTER
6 tablespoons (3 oz/90 g) unsalted butter

3 ounces (90 g) bittersweet chocolate, chopped
1 egg
2 egg yolks
1/4 cup (2 oz/60 g) sugar
1/2 cup (2 1/2 oz/75 g) all-purpose flour

WHITE CHOCOLATE BATTER
6 tablespoons (3 oz/90 g) unsalted butter

3 ounces (90 g) white chocolate, chopped
1 egg
2 egg yolks
1/4 cup (2 oz/60 g) sugar
1/2 cup (2 1/2 oz/75 g) all-purpose flour

RASPBERRY SAUCE
2 cups (8 oz/250 g) fresh raspberries
1/4 cup (2 oz/60 g) sugar
1/4 cup (2 fl oz/60 ml) water

- Preheat the oven to 325°F (165°C). Butter six 3-inch (7.5-cm) ramekins.
- To make the dark chocolate batter: In a medium saucepan, melt the butter over low heat. Remove from heat and stir in the chocolate until it melts. Set aside.
- In a medium bowl, using an electric mixer, beat the egg, egg yolks, and sugar on medium speed for 2 minutes. Increase the speed to high and beat for another 2 minutes. Reduce speed to low and continue to beat until a slowly dissolving ribbon forms on the surface of the batter when the beaters are lifted.
- Gradually fold in the flour. Fold in the dark chocolate mixture until blended.
- To make the white chocolate batter: Repeat the same procedure as for the dark chocolate batter.
- Spoon 1 heaping tablespoon of the white chocolate batter into the prepared ramekins. Spoon the dark chocolate batter on top to fill the ramekins three-fourths full. Top with white chocolate batter. Bake in the preheated oven for 15 minutes, or until the top springs back when pressed.
- To make the raspberry sauce: In a small saucepan, simmer the water and sugar until the sugar is dissolved. Add the raspberries and cook for 10 minutes.
- To serve, spoon a pool of raspberry sauce on each of 6 plates and place a warm cake in the center. *Makes 6 individual cakes*

DENVER ART MUSEUM
DENVER, COLORADO

As a region, Denver has a tremendously high quality of life, which is sustained and enriched by organizations like the Denver Art Museum, both culturally and economically. By providing education, enrichment, and economic stability, the Denver Art Museum is one of Denver's most prized masterpieces.

—Joe Blake, President/CEO
Denver Metro Chamber of Commerce

F ounded in 1893, the Denver Art Museum (DAM) has assembled a comprehensive collection and is the largest encyclopedic museum between Kansas City and the West Coast. In 1971, the museum moved into an astounding twenty-eight-sided building designed by Italian architect Gio Ponti. The building's exterior is covered with more than one million faceted, shimmering tiles, and its two 7-story towers provide a nontraditional museum-going experience. Visitors can use elevators to move quickly between seven floors of small galleries and thus avoid the syndrome known as museum fatigue. The Denver museum is currently planning a striking new wing in glass and titanium designed by Daniel Libeskind. The expansion is scheduled for completion in 2005.

Highlights of Denver's permanent collections include European and American painting and sculpture; Spanish Colonial and Pre-Columbian art; Art of the American West; and contemporary art. The collections includes paintings by Claude Monet, Mary Cassatt, Georgia O'Keeffe, Henri Matisse, and Pablo Picasso; and the spirit of the American West is captured in works by Frederic Remington, Charles Marion Russell, and Albert Bierstadt among others. Contemporary pieces include Deborah Butterfield's sculptured horse *Orion* and Jim Dine's *Wheatfield*.

The museum's internationally renowned collection of Native American art includes artistic traditions across North America, including Pueblo pottery, Navajo weavings, Plains beadwork, Eskimo ivories, and a growing collection of contemporary works. The museum's spectacular American Indian costume collection, donated to the museum by curator Frederic Douglass, has influenced fashion design and brought Native American art to the attention of the American public.

AMADEO MODIGLIANI *Portrait of A Woman* 1918

Encouraging art appreciation among young people is a priority for the museum. In the European and American Art galleries, a Discovery Library encourages children to rummage through artifacts or dress up like specific subjects portrayed in various paintings. Art Stops located throughout the galleries demonstrate how Navajo Indians weave blankets; how bronze sculptures are cast; and why dragons, bats, and flowers appear on Chinese silk robes. Classes and workshops for children and adults are regular features on the museum calendar.

At the museum's award-winning Palettes restaurant, chef Kevin Taylor's fresh interpretations of American cuisine are served in an elegant, contemporary setting. His flavorful dishes are often based on current museum exhibitions. Palettes is open for lunch and for Wednesday-evening dinners, when the museum stays open late. For quick, buffet-style meals, Palette Express offers salads, soups, pastas, and sandwiches. The following recipes were created by native Coloradan Kevin Taylor, Palettes' chef and owner.

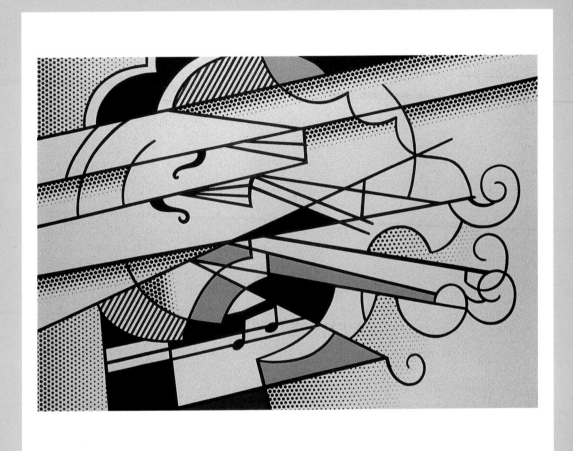

ROY LICHTENSTEIN *The Violin* 1976

VICHYSSOISE WITH MARINATED LEEKS

In 1910, chef Louis Diat created vichyssoise at the New York Ritz-Carlton Hotel in memory of the leek and potato soup he had enjoyed while growing up in Vichy, France.

4 Yukon Gold potatoes

6 cups (48 fl oz/1.5 l) half-and-half

$^1/_2$ teaspoon saffron threads

$^1/_4$ teaspoon cayenne pepper

2 teaspoons Tabasco sauce

$1^1/_2$ teaspoons Worcestershire sauce

1 tablespoon salt

Marinated Leeks (recipe follows)

■ Put the potatoes in a large pot and add water to cover by 2 inches (7-cm). Bring to a boil, reduce heat to low, and simmer for 30 minutes, or until tender when pierced with a knife. Drain and let cool. Use your fingers to rub off the skins.

■ Push the potatoes through a ricer or mash them with a potato masher in a medium saucepan. Stir in the half-and-half, saffron, and cayenne; bring to a simmer over medium heat and cook for 5 to 10 minutes. Transfer to a blender or food processor and purée. Transfer to a large bowl and stir in the Tabasco, Worcestershire, and salt. Let cool. Refrigerate for at least 1 hour, or until chilled. Ladle into bowls and top with marinated leeks. *Makes 6 servings*

MARINATED LEEKS

3 tablespoons olive oil

$^1/_2$ teaspoon freshly ground pepper

2 teaspoons minced fresh thyme

2 teaspoons packed brown sugar

1 teaspoon salt

2 tablespoons Champagne or white wine vinegar

1 tablespoon fresh lemon juice

3 leeks, white part only, thinly sliced

■ In a small bowl, combine all the ingredients except the leeks. Whisk to blend.

■ In a pot of salted boiling water, blanch the leeks for about 10 seconds; drain. Stir the leeks into the vinaigrette. Let cool. Refrigerate for at least 1 hour, or until chilled.

SEA BASS WITH ROASTED POTATOES, BRAISED FENNEL, AND BOUILLABAISSE SAUCE

Complementary and contrasting tastes and textures are perfectly balanced in this outstanding dish. Swordfish or halibut may be substituted for the sea bass.

2 cups (16 fl oz/500 ml) chicken stock (see Basics) or canned low-salt chicken broth

2 fennel bulbs, trimmed and cored

4 tablespoons (2 fl oz/60 ml) olive oil

8 fingerling, creamer, or small red or white potatoes

4 sea bass fillets

Bouillabaisse Sauce (recipe follows)

Salt and freshly ground pepper to taste

■ In a medium saucepan, combine the stock or broth and fennel over medium-low heat. Cover and cook for 30 minutes, or until soft. Drain and let cool. Cut the fennel into matchsticks and set aside.

■ Preheat the oven to 400°F (200°C). Oil the bottom of a 9-by-13-inch (23-by-33-cm) baking dish with 1 tablespoon of the olive oil. In a pot of salted boiling water, cook the potatoes for 10 minutes, or until tender but still firm; drain and let cool. Cut each potato in half and arrange, cut side down, in the prepared dish. Bake in the preheated oven for 20 minutes, or until the potatoes are browned and crisp.

■ In a large ovenproof frying pan, add the remaining 3 tablespoons olive oil and heat until it shimmers. Add the fish fillets and cook for about 1 minute on each side, or until golden brown. Transfer the pan to the preheated oven and bake for 5 to 6 minutes, or until the fish is opaque throughout.

■ To serve, arrange a mound of fennel in the center of each of 4 plates and top with a fish fillet. Arrange 4 potato halves around each plate, ladle bouillabaisse sauce around the fish, and serve immediately. *Makes 4 servings*

(continued)

BOUILLABAISSE SAUCE

1 tablespoon olive oil

4 shallots, minced

$^1/_2$ fennel bulb, trimmed, cored, and
   cut into matchsticks

2 garlic cloves, sliced

Pinch of saffron threads

2 tomatoes, chopped

1 cup (8 fl oz/250 ml) dry white wine

2 cups (16 fl oz/500 ml) fish stock
   (see Basics) or canned low-salt
   chicken broth

1 bay leaf

Pinch of grated orange zest

1 star anise pod

Salt and freshly ground pepper to taste

2 tablespoons extra-virgin olive oil

■ In a large frying pan over medium heat, heat the olive oil and sauté the shallots, fennel, garlic, and saffron for 3 minutes. Add the tomatoes, wine, stock or broth, and bay leaf and simmer for 1 hour. Stir in the orange zest and star anise and simmer for 5 minutes. Remove the star anise and bay leaf. Transfer the sauce to a blender or food processor and purée. Season with salt and pepper. With the machine running, gradually add the 2 tablespoons extra-virgin olive oil and blend until emulsified. *Makes about 3 cups (24 fl oz/750 ml)*

Southwestern American Indian gallery

WILLARD LEROY METCALF *The Ten Cent Breakfast* 1887

WARM BITTERSWEET CHOCOLATE CAKES

Rich and luscious, these individual cakes have soft centers and are topped with chocolate ganache.

^{1}/2 cup (4 fl oz/125 ml) heavy cream

1 tablespoon unsweetened cocoa
   powder

2 tablespoons unsalted butter

5 ounces (155 g) bittersweet chocolate, chopped

2 eggs, separated

^{1}/4 cup (2 oz/60 g) sugar

^{1}/4 cup (1 oz/30 g) ground pecans

1 teaspoon vanilla extract

GANACHE TOPPING

2 tablespoons heavy cream

1 ounce (30 g) bittersweet chocolate,
   chopped

Vanilla ice cream for serving

■ Preheat the oven to 350°F (180°C). Butter six 3-inch (7.5-cm) ramekins and sprinkle with sugar.

■ In a heavy, medium saucepan, combine the cream, cocoa powder, and butter. Bring just to a boil over medium heat. Remove from heat and stir in the choco-late until it melts. Stir in the egg yolks until well blended.

■ In a large bowl, beat the egg whites and sugar until stiff, glossy peaks form. Stir the pecans into the chocolate mixture and fold in the egg whites.

■ Fill the prepared ramekins two-thirds full with the batter. Bake in preheated oven for 15 to 20 minutes, or until a knife inserted in the center of a ramekin comes out almost clean. Remove from oven and let cool in the ramekins for 10 minutes, then unmold.

■ Meanwhile, make the ganache topping: In a small saucepan, bring the cream to a boil over medium heat. Remove from heat and stir in the chocolate until it melts. Let cool, stirring occasionally to prevent a skin from forming. Frost the top of each cake with the ganache.

■ Serve the cakes warm, with a scoop of vanilla ice cream on the side. *Makes 6 individual cakes*

THE J. PAUL GETTY MUSEUM
LOS ANGELES, CALIFORNIA

The Getty Museum, as far as I know, is the only museum in America, if not in the world,
in which the visitor has the ability to look at art in the galleries and then walk out to the
gardens and in a free and unproscribed manner move back into the galleries . . . Being at
The Getty Center is a different enlightening experience for each visitor that goes there, one
that refers to both the art and the art of architecture. —Richard Meier, Architect

L andscape, light, and architecture all come together at the Getty Center to create an unforgettable setting for viewing some of the world's greatest art treasures. Perched on a hilltop above Los Angeles in the foothills of the Santa Monica Mountains, The Getty has welcomed over six million people since its opening in 1997. Visitors enter at the main gate and then ascend in a computer-operated tram through the dry, spare landscape of a Southern California canyon before arriving at the Center's open campus.

The five pavilions that make up the museum are just part of the J. Paul Getty Center, a complex designed by Pritzker Prize–winning American architect Richard Meier to include buildings for research and administration as well as public galleries. His design makes the most of a climate where the outdoors is accessible most of the year, and visitors can walk inside and out between galleries and gardens. The buildings, walkways, and courtyards are clad in gorgeous travertine stone quarried in Italy. A visit to the Central Garden created by Robert Irwin is a must. Streams, trees, azaleas, and gurgling pools provide a serene setting for views of sky, hills, and the blue Pacific beyond.

At the Getty, art can be viewed either chronologically or in random sequence by moving between pavilions. Paintings are displayed under natural light in skylit galleries, and the museum's collection of French decorative arts and furniture is housed in a series of period rooms. The museum's permanent collection includes paintings by major artists, including Rembrandt, Fragonard, Van Gogh, Monet, and Cézanne; some of the world's finest illuminated manuscripts; drawings by masters such as Michelangelo, Raphael, and Degas; European sculpture and

GERRIT VAN HONTHORST *Musical Group on a Balcony* 1622

antiquities, and a collection of photographs that is regarded as among the best in the world.

The Getty's Education Department offers programs for children, families, seniors, students, and scholars. Displays, hands-on activities, and games are available in English and Spanish to help young people make connections with the exhibits in the galleries. Other public programs include the Gordon Getty Concerts, a series that complements current museum exhibitions; and Friday Nights at the Getty, free performances by award-winning writers, actors, and musicians.

Dining options at The Getty include the Cafe, with cafeteria-style service for lunch and indoor/outdoor seating; the Garden Terrace Cafe, with self-service snacks and simple lunches on a terrace overlooking the Central Garden; and a picnic area. The Restaurant at The Getty offers acclaimed California cuisine with Mediterranean and Asian influences, a tasting menu, and dishes inspired by current exhibitions. A large mural by Los Angeles–based artist Alexis Smith is a focal point of the elegant room, and an outdoor terrace has stunning views of the Santa Monica Mountains and the Pacific Ocean. The following recipes were created by chef Terri Buzzard and pastry chef Jim Dodge.

NIKODEMOS (POTTER) *Panathenaic Prize Amphora with Lid* 363–362 B.C.

GAZPACHO

No cooking is required to make this cool summertime soup. Serve as a refreshing starter for dinner, or for lunch on a hot day.

4 tomatoes
1 small jicama, peeled and chopped
1 cucumber, peeled and chopped
$^1/_4$ cup (1 oz/30 g) diced white onion
2 garlic cloves, chopped
$^1/_4$ cup (2 fl oz/60 ml) olive oil

$^1/_2$ cup (4 fl oz/125 ml) rice vinegar
1 teaspoon cumin seeds, toasted
  (see Basics)
Tabasco sauce to taste
Salt and freshly ground pepper
  to taste

■ In a blender or food processor, combine all the ingredients and purée. Refrigerate for at least 2 hours to give the flavors time to blend. Ladle the soup into chilled soup bowls or mugs. *Makes 8 to 10 servings*

JEAN ANTOINE WATTEAU *Two Studies of a Flutist and a Study of the Head of a Boy* c. 1716–1719

CORN CAKES WITH WHIPPED GOAT CHEESE

These delicate little cakes are topped with fluffy, lightly-herbed goat cheese.

WHIPPED GOAT CHEESE

$1/2$ cup (4 oz/125 g) fresh white goat
  cheese at room temperature
$1^1/2$ tablespoons sour cream or plain
  yogurt
1 teaspoon minced fresh thyme or
  rosemary
Salt and freshly ground pepper to taste
1 teaspoon olive oil

CORN CAKES

2 eggs
$1^1/4$ cups ($7^1/2$ oz/235 g) fresh corn
  kernels
$1/2$ cup ($2^1/2$ oz/75 g) stone-ground
  cornmeal
$1/2$ teaspoon salt
$1/4$ teaspoon freshly ground pepper
$1/4$ cup (1 oz/30 g) chopped green
  onions, white part only
2 egg whites

Canola oil for filming pan
Minced fresh flat-leaf parsley for
  garnish

■ In a medium bowl, combine all the whipped goat cheese ingredients. Using an electric mixer, beat together until light and fluffy.

■ To make the corn cakes: In a blender or food processor, combine the eggs and $3/4$ cup (4 oz/125 g) of the corn kernels. Purée until smooth. Transfer the purée to a large bowl and stir in the cornmeal, salt, pepper, green onions, and remaining corn kernels.

■ In a medium bowl, beat the egg whites until stiff, glossy peaks form. Fold the egg whites into the corn mixture.

■ Heat a griddle or large skillet over medium heat and oil it lightly. Drop the batter by heaping tablespoons and cook until bubbles appear evenly on the surface, about 1 minute. Turn and cook for 1 minute on the other side, or until golden.

■ Arrange 2 or 3 pancakes on each of 4 plates and top with a dollop of whipped goat cheese. Sprinkle with parsley and serve immediately. *Makes 4 servings*

Halibut with Braised Artichoke Hearts, Yukon Gold Potatoes, and Meyer Lemon Vinaigrette

Make this dish with the freshest of fish in early spring, when Meyer lemons and artichokes are in season. The artichoke bottoms may be cooked 1 day ahead; cover them with the reserved stock or broth and refrigerate.

2 large artichokes

4 cups (32 fl oz/1 l) chicken stock (see Basics) or canned low-salt chicken broth

8 small Yukon Gold potatoes

4 tablespoons olive oil, plus more for coating

2 garlic cloves, minced

Salt and freshly ground pepper to taste

4 halibut fillets

$^1/_2$ cup (1/2 oz/15 g) fresh basil leaves, chopped

Meyer Lemon Vinaigrette

$^1/_3$ cup (3 fl oz/80 ml) fresh Meyer lemon juice*

$^1/_3$ cup (3 fl oz/80 ml) white wine vinegar

$^1/_3$ cup (3 fl oz/80 ml) extra-virgin olive oil

Salt and freshly ground pepper to taste

Garnish

$^1/_4$ cup (1 oz/30 g) thinly sliced green onions (white part only)

2 tomatoes, seeded and diced

■ Using a sharp knife, trim the leaves from the artichokes, leaving the heart and stem. Peel the stems and use a teaspoon to scoop out the chokes. Immediately transfer the artichokes to a medium saucepan and add the stock or broth. Cover and bring to a slow simmer over medium-low heat. Continue cooking until tender, 30 to 40 minutes. Using a slotted spoon, transfer the artichoke hearts to a bowl and let cool. Cut into $^3/_4$-inch (2-cm) dice and set aside.

■ Preheat the oven to 375°F (190°C). Cut each potato into 4 or 5 rounds. In a medium bowl, toss the potatoes with 3 tablespoons of the olive oil, the garlic, salt, and pepper. Arrange the slices in a single layer on a baking sheet and bake for 25 minutes, or until golden brown. Remove from the oven and set aside.

■ Coat each halibut fillet with olive oil and sprinkle with salt. In a large ovenproof frying pan over medium-high heat, sauté the fillets until golden brown on each side. Place the pan in the oven and bake for 10 minutes, or until the fish is opaque.

- In a large frying pan over medium-high heat, heat the remaining 1 tablespoon olive oil and sauté the artichoke hearts and the potatoes until heated through. Stir in the basil and season with salt and pepper.
- In a small bowl, whisk together all the vinaigrette ingredients.
- Arrange a mound of artichokes and potatoes on each of 4 plates. Top with a halibut fillet and sprinkle the tomatoes and green onions around the fish. Drizzle generously with the vinaigrette and serve at once. *Makes 4 servings*

* Thin-skinned Meyer lemons have a relatively low-acid juice with a lemon-orange flavor; if Meyer lemons are not available, use 1/4 cup fresh regular lemon juice.

JACOB VAN HULSDONCK *Still Life with Lemons, Oranges, and a Pomegranate* c. 1620–1640

LEMON TART WITH BLACKBERRY SAUCE

Lemon and chocolate are a deliciously rich combination, and the blackberry sauce makes a stunning visual and flavor contrast. Prepare this tart at 6 least hours before you plan to serve it.

PASTRY
1¹/4 cups (6¹/2 oz/220 g) all-purpose flour
¹/2 teaspoon sugar
¹/4 teaspoon salt
¹/2 cup (4 oz/125 g) cold unsalted butter, thinly sliced
¹/4 cup (2 fl oz/60 ml) heavy cream

FILLING
1 cup (8 fl oz/250 ml) heavy cream
3 large eggs
¹/2 cup (4 oz/125 g) sugar
¹/3 cup (3 fl oz/80 ml) fresh lemon juice
4 ounces (125 g) white chocolate, chopped

BLACKBERRY SAUCE
4 cups (16 oz/500 g) fresh blackberries, rinsed and dried
¹/4 cup (2¹/2 oz/75 g) corn syrup

■ To make the pastry: In a food processor, combine the flour, sugar, and salt. Process until blended. Add the butter and process to the consistency of coarse meal. Pour in the cream and process until the dough just comes together.

■ On a lightly floured board, briefly knead the dough and flatten into a disk. Roll the dough out into a round 11 inches (25 cm) in diameter. Line a 9-inch (23-cm) tart pan with the dough, trim the edges, and refrigerate for 2 hours.

■ Preheat the oven to 350°F (180°C). Place the oven rack on the bottom shelf of the oven. Line the crust with aluminum foil. Use the tines of a fork to press holes through the foil and dough, spacing them 1/2 inch (12 mm) apart and covering the bottom. Bake the pastry in the preheated oven for 30 to 35 minutes, or until light golden brown. Remove from the oven and let cool on a wire rack for 15 minutes. Carefully remove the foil and let the pastry cool for 1 hour.

■ To make the filling: In a deep bowl, beat the cream until firm peaks form. Cover with plastic wrap and refrigerate.

■ In a double boiler or stainless-steel bowl over barely simmering water, whisk the eggs constantly until pale. Add the sugar and lemon juice and whisk constantly until the lemon curd thickens to resemble pudding. Remove from heat; if the eggs get too hot, they will scramble. Stir in the white chocolate until it melts. Set aside and let cool.

■ Fold the cooled lemon curd into the whipped cream. Pour the filling into the pre-baked tart shell, spreading the top evenly. Cover the tart with plastic wrap and refrigerate for at least 6 hours or as long as overnight before serving.

■ In a blender or food processor, combine the ingredients for the blackberry sauce; purée. Strain the sauce though a fine-meshed sieve into a bowl and refrigerate until ready to serve.

■ To serve, cut the tart into 8 wedges. Ladle a pool of blackberry sauce onto each of 8 plates and top with a slice of tart. *Makes 8 servings*

WILLIAM JAMES GLACKENS *Still Life with Roses and Fruit* c. 1924

The High Museum of Art
Atlanta, Georgia

I live in Atlanta and have always been treated well as a resident here. I love the High Museum . . . it's a great building. I was able to show my photography collection here and it was nice to do it in a town that has shown me so much love and opened its arms to me. The High Museum was the perfect place to show what I've been collecting while living here.

—Sir Elton John

Atlanta's High Museum of Art (the High), the Southeast's premier art museum, is known for an extensive permanent collection displayed in a thematic rather than a chronological fashion. The High's deputy director and chief curator, Michael E. Shapiro, explains why: "Art should be accessible to everyone, not just the critic or the collector. We hope that by breaking from the customary chronological, academic arrangement, we can help all museum visitors enjoy our permanent collection in a new way."

The High's collections include significant holdings in nineteenth- and twentieth-century American art; an acclaimed collection of decorative arts; European paintings, including Italian art from the fourteenth through the eighteenth centuries, and Impressionist and Post-Impressionist masterpieces; folk art; and a growing collection of photography. The High also regularly sponsors ambitious exhibitions from major museums worldwide.

Founded in 1905 as the Atlanta Art Association, the High received its first permanent location, as well as its name, from Hattie High, who donated her family's home to the fledgling museum. Today, the museum is housed in a spectacular building designed by architect Richard Meier. The museum is part of the Woodruff Arts Center, along with other Atlanta cultural institutions including the Atlanta Symphony Orchestra. Already the center of Atlanta's thriving arts community, the Woodruff Center and the High Museum are currently in the midst of an expansion that will create more gallery and public space for the museum and an integrated presence in an exciting Arts Center campus. Pritzker Prize–winning Italian architect Renzo Piano will create the museum expansion plan and the Woodruff Arts Center's architectural master plan.

Visitors to the High can gain an understanding of the basic elements of art in a special interactive gallery in the Visual Arts Learning Space. Other programs for adults include films, lectures, workshops, and the High Noon series, which presents artists, art historians, and musicians at midday events. One of the many educational programs sponsored by the High is the Metro-Atlanta Partnership for the Visual Arts and Learning, which links visual and verbal learning in Atlanta schools. Atlanta-area families can also take advantage of an array of activities for children, including Toddler Thursdays, Saturday Workshops, and Art Camps for older children.

The following recipes were created by chef Christophe Holmes of Legendary Events, an award-winning catering firm that plans all special events at the High. Hungry museum visitors can also enjoy sandwiches, soups, salads, and baked goods at Alon's Café.

AMALIA AMAKI *Les Enfants* 1999

GRILLED LAMB CHOPS

These chops are incredibly tasty on the outdoor grill, but they can also be broiled. Salting the chops in advance helps to heighten flavor and retain the natural juices. Venison chops can be substituted for the lamb.

$^{1}/_{4}$ cup (2 oz/60 g) salt

2 tablespoons freshly ground pepper

$^{1}/_{2}$ cup ($^{3}/_{4}$ oz/20 g) organic lavender

$^{1}/_{4}$ cup ($^{1}/_{3}$ oz/10 g) minced fresh thyme

4 double-thick loin lamb chops

■ In a shallow dish, combine the salt, pepper, lavender, and thyme. Press the salt mixture into the lamb chops so they are well coated. Cover and refrigerate for 12 to 24 hours. Remove from the refrigerator 30 minutes before grilling.

■ Light a fire in a charcoal grill. Grill the chops over high heat, about 4 minutes per side for medium rare. Serve immediately, with Bulgur Pilaf and Sautéed Haricots Verts (following). *Makes 4 servings*

BULGUR PILAF

This satisfying side dish has a nutty flavor and chewy texture. Barley may be substituted for the bulgur.

4 tablespoons (2 oz/60 g) unsalted butter or $^{1}/_{4}$ cup (2 fl oz/60 ml) olive oil

1 small onion, diced

$1^{1}/_{2}$ cups (10 oz/300 g) bulgur wheat

1 bay leaf

4 cups (32 fl oz/1 l) chicken stock (see Basics) or canned low-salt broth, heated

Salt and freshly ground pepper to taste

■ In a large frying pan, melt the butter or heat the olive oil over medium heat. Sauté the onion for 5 minutes, or until translucent. Stir in the bulgur and bay leaf and sauté for 1 minute. Add the stock or broth, salt, and pepper. Reduce heat to low, cover, and cook for 15 minutes, or until the liquid is absorbed. Remove the bay leaf and fluff the bulgur with a fork before serving. *Makes 4 servings*

SAUTÉED HARICOTS VERTS
SAUTÉED FRENCH GREEN BEANS

Thin, tender green beans are quickly prepared and perfect with grilled lamb chops.

$^{1}/_{4}$ cup (2 oz/60 g) unsalted butter
2 garlic cloves, minced
1 pound (16 oz/500 g) haricots verts
   (French green beans)

$^{1}/_{3}$ cup (3 fl oz/80 ml) water
Salt and freshly ground pepper
   to taste

■ In a large frying pan, melt the butter over medium heat and sauté the garlic for 2 minutes, or until golden. Add the green beans and sauté for 1 minute. Pour in the water and cook for 3 minutes, or until the water evaporates and the beans are crisp-tender. Season with salt and pepper. *Makes 4 servings*

MATTIE LOU O'KELLEY *Spring Vegetable Scene* 1968

THE HIGH MUSEUM OF ART

WHITE CHOCOLATE BREAD PUDDING WITH JACK DANIELS SAUCE

A comforting dessert dressed up with luscious white chocolate and a grown-up sauce.

$^1/_2$ cup (4 fl oz/125 ml) brandy

$^1/_2$ cup (4 oz/125 g) raisins

12 slices day-old white bread, cut into cubes

4 cups (32 fl oz/1 l) heavy cream or half-and-half

4 eggs

$1^1/_2$ cups (12 oz/375 g) sugar

2 tablespoons vanilla extract

4 tablespoons (2 oz/60 g) unsalted butter, melted

8 ounces (250 g) white chocolate, shaved

Jack Daniels Sauce (recipe follows)

■ Preheat the oven to 350°F (180°C). Butter a 9-by-13-inch (23-by-33-cm) baking dish.

■ In a medium saucepan, combine the brandy and raisins and bring to a simmer over medium-low heat. Remove from heat and set aside for 30 minutes.

■ Put the bread cubes in a medium bowl and pour the cream or half-and-half over; set aside.

■ In a large bowl, beat the eggs and sugar together until pale and thick. Stir in the vanilla, melted butter, brandy, and raisins. Add the bread mixture and chocolate shavings and stir until blended. Pour into the prepared baking dish and bake in the preheated oven for 45 minutes, or until the pudding is golden brown and a knife inserted into the center comes out almost clean. Remove from the oven and let cool slightly or completely. Serve the pudding warm or at room temperature with a little Jack Daniels sauce spooned over each serving. *Makes 6 to 8 servings*

JACK DANIELS SAUCE

$^1/_2$ cup (4 oz/125 g) unsalted butter

1 cup (8 oz/250 g) sugar

1 egg

$^1/_2$ cup (4 fl oz/125 ml) Jack Daniels whiskey

■ In a medium saucepan, melt the butter over low heat; remove from heat.

■ In a medium bowl, beat the sugar and egg together until pale. Pour in the Jack Daniels and beat until mixed. Add the melted butter and beat until thick and creamy. Serve warm. *Makes about $1^1/_4$ cups (10 fl oz/310 ml)*

RUFINO TAMAYO *Woman with Fruit Basket* 1926

LOS ANGELES COUNTY MUSEUM OF ART
LOS ANGELES, CALIFORNIA

Los Angeles is such a modern city, fresh, exciting, and constantly changing. Everyone is very aware of the rising stars of the most recent fashion. LACMA reflects this modernity without forgetting the values and cultures that have contributed to building this complex city.
—Sister Wendy Beckett

The Los Angeles County Museum of Art (LACMA) is the premier encyclopedic art museum in the western United States and reflects the many heritages and cultural communities of Southern California. With its five separate buildings, a central courtyard, open walkways, and eclectic architecture, the museum has an open, friendly atmosphere, perfect to enjoy on a typically warm and sunny Los Angeles afternoon.

In 1961, the trustees and staff of the city's Museum of Science, History, and Art decided to create an independent museum devoted to the history of visual art. The Los Angeles County Museum of Art opened in 1965 at its current site on Wilshire Boulevard. The museum's many strengths include American and European painting and sculpture; ancient and Islamic art; and Latin American art, including the world's largest collection of works by Rufino Tamayo. To present its vast and diverse collection, LACMA develops special exhibitions that highlight a certain period, locale, artist, or style. The museum's dramatic Pavilion for Japanese Art was designed by Bruce Goff to showcase a significant collection of Japanese scrolls, paintings, prints, textiles, and *netsuke*, tiny Japanese sculptures. In December 2001, LACMA announced that acclaimed Dutch architect Rem Koolhaas has been chosen to design a new space for the museum at its existing site. Koolhaas' design will encourage museum goers to move through LACMA's permanent collection, making connections between various periods and styles or exploring the art of one time and place in depth.

LACMA's acclaimed music program offers a wide variety of concerts. Monday Evening Concerts present new and innovative works; the Rosalind Gilbert Concerts offer classical and baroque programs; and Friday Evening Jazz at the Museum has become a popular and permanent part of the schedule. The museum's commitment to education and outreach is evident in programs such as the Maya

Mobile, a forty-eight-foot classroom on wheels for Los Angeles–area sixth-graders, and the LACMA Institute for Art and Cultures, which brings together artists, writers, and performers to explore the relationship of the arts to broader cultural and social issues.

Museum visitors can stop at the Plaza Cafe for cafeteria-style snacks or dine in the stylish Pentimento restaurant just off the central courtyard in the Hammer Building. Executive chef Joachim Splichal's menu of innovative appetizers, entrée salads, and desserts is served in an airy, contemporary setting. Outdoor patio seating is especially popular on Friday evenings, when LACMA's jazz concerts take place in the Times Mirror Central Court.

Woman with a Lute c. 1600–1610

ROASTED GARLIC AND SUN-DRIED-TOMATO HUMMUS

Serve this flavorful vegetarian dip with crisp raw vegetables, pita bread, or crostini.

14½-ounces (455 g) canned garbanzo beans, drained and rinsed

8 roasted garlic cloves, plus a few more for garnish (see Basics)

2 tablespoons fresh lemon juice

½ teaspoon salt

¼ cup (2 1/2 oz/75 g) tahini (sesame paste)

¼ cup (2 fl oz/60 ml) olive oil

2 tablespoons minced fresh flat-leaf parsley, plus more for garnish

About ¼ cup (2 fl oz/60 ml) water

½ cup (4 oz/125 g) oil-packed sun-dried tomatoes, drained and finely chopped

Crostini (see Basics) for serving

■ In a blender or food processor, combine the garbanzo beans, the 8 roasted garlic cloves, lemon juice, salt, tahini, olive oil, and the 2 tablespoons parsley. Blend until smooth, adding water as necessary until the hummus is creamy. Transfer to a bowl and stir in the sun-dried tomatoes. Garnish with parsley and roasted garlic cloves. *Makes about 1½ cups (12 fl oz/375 ml)*

ROASTED CORN AND POBLANO CHOWDER

Roasted corn and poblano chilies give this soup a fresh, new taste.

4 ears fresh corn, shucked

4 cups (32 fl oz/1 l) half and half

1 tablespoon cumin seeds

1 bay leaf

1 teaspoon ground nutmeg

1 sprig fresh rosemary

2 tablespoons olive oil or unsalted
butter

1 onion, diced

1 teaspoon salt or to taste

2 garlic cloves, minced

1 teaspoon ground cumin

1 small red bell pepper, seeded,
deribbed, and diced

3 poblano chilies or 2 small green bell
peppers, roasted, peeled, and diced
(see Basics)

2 small red potatoes, peeled and diced

Chopped fresh chives for garnish

- Preheat the oven to 450°F (230°C). Wrap each ear of corn tightly in aluminum foil. Place in a shallow baking dish and bake in the preheated oven for 20 minutes. Remove from the oven and let cool. Remove the foil and cut off the kernels.
- In a medium saucepan, combine the half-and-half, cumin seeds, bay leaf, nutmeg, and rosemary. Bring to a simmer over low heat. Remove from heat and let infuse for 20 minutes, or to taste.
- In a large saucepan, heat the olive oil or melt the butter over low heat and sauté the onion with the salt for 15 to 20 minutes, or until golden brown. Add the garlic and ground cumin and sauté for 5 minutes. Stir in the corn kernels, red bell pepper, and poblanos or bell peppers and sauté for 5 minutes. Pour the infused half-and-half through a fine-mesh sieve into the soup and simmer for 10 to 15 minutes.
- Transfer 3 cups (24 fl oz/750 ml) of the soup to a food processor or blender and purée. Stir the purée back into the soup. Add the potatoes and simmer for 5 to 10 minutes, or until soft. Ladle the soup into bowls, garnish with chives, and serve immediately. *Makes 6 to 8 servings*

PENTIMENTO SAUSAGE LASAGNA

Italian sausage, radicchio, Italian cheeses, and a tomato sauce flavored with fresh herbs blend in this trusty, make-ahead party dish.

4 tablespoons (2 fl oz/60 ml) olive oil

1 pound (500 g) mild Italian sausage

2 onions, diced

3 to 4 garlic cloves, minced

1 cup (8 fl oz/250 ml) dry white wine

24 Roma (plum) tomatoes, peeled and chopped

3 cups (24 fl oz/750 ml) tomato juice

1/4 cup (1/4 oz/7 g) minced fresh basil

1/4 cup (1/4 oz/7 g) minced fresh oregano

1/4 cup (1/4 oz/7 oz) minced fresh thyme

2 bay leaves

Salt and freshly ground pepper to taste

Dash of sugar

8 leaves (1 small head) radicchio

Two 8-ounce (250-g) packages "oven-ready" lasagna noodles

1 1/2 cups (8 oz/250 g) crumbled ricotta salata cheese*

4 cups (1 lb/500 g) shredded fontina cheese

■ In large, heavy saucepan over medium heat, heat 2 tablespoons of the olive oil. Add the sausages and cook for about 15 minutes, or until browned on all sides. Transfer the sausages to a plate and set aside. Add the onions and garlic to the saucepan and sauté for 3 to 4 minutes, or until the onion is translucent. Pour in the wine and stir to scrape up any browned bits on the bottom of the pan. Increase heat to medium-high and cook, stirring occasionally, for 3 minutes, or until reduced to a glaze.

■ Stir in the tomatoes, tomato juice, basil, oregano, thyme, bay leaves, salt, pepper, and sugar. Bring to a boil, reduce heat to low, and simmer for 30 minutes, stirring occasionally. Meanwhile, slice the sausages and add them to the sauce.

■ Preheat the oven to 350°F (180°C). In a small ovenproof baking dish, combine the radicchio, salt and pepper to taste, and the remaining 2 tablespoons olive oil. Sprinkle with salt and pepper. Toss to coat. Bake in the preheated oven for 5 minutes, or until the radicchio wilts. Remove from the oven, leaving the oven on, and set aside to cool.

(continued)

■ Remove the bay leaves from the sauce. In a 9-by-13-inch (23-by-33-cm) baking dish, spread a thin layer of the sauce and arrange a layer of pasta sheets on top. Sprinkle with $^1/_2$ cup ($2^1/_2$ oz/75 g) of the ricotta salata and $^1/_4$ cup (1 oz/30 g) of the fontina. Top with a second layer of pasta sheets and a second layer of sauce. Cover with the radicchio and sprinkle with more ricotta salata. Top with a third layer of pasta and cover with more sauce, ricotta salata, and fontina. Arrange a fourth layer of pasta on top and cover with the remaining sauce. Top with the remaining fontina.

■ Cover with aluminum foil and bake in the preheated oven for 45 minutes, or until hot and bubbling. Remove the foil and increase the oven temperature to 450°F (230°C). Bake for 15 minutes, or until the cheese is golden brown. Remove from the oven and let stand for 10 minutes before cutting into squares and serving. *Makes 8 to 10 servings*

* Ricotta salata, a dry, aged version of fresh ricotta, is a salty, firm white sheep's milk cheese. It is available at many cheese stores, specialty foods stores, and Italian markets. Parmesan or pecorino may be substituted.

PINEAPPLE-MANGO TARTE TATIN

A marvelous twist on the classic French caramelized upside-down apple tart.

3/4 cup (6 oz/185 g) sugar

1/4 cup (2 fl oz/60 ml) water

1/4 fresh pineapple (cut from center), peeled, cored, and cut into thin slices

1 mango, peeled and cut from the pit in 2 thick slices

Four 3 1/2-inch (9-cm) rounds thawed frozen puff pastry, pricked with a fork

Raspberry Coulis for serving (page 98)

Fruit sorbet for serving (optional)

■ Preheat the oven to 350°F (180°C). In a small, heavy saucepan over high heat, combine the sugar and water. Bring to a boil and cook until deep golden brown. Remove from heat and quickly pour the caramel into four 3 1/2-inch (9-cm) ramekins. Arrange the pineapple decoratively over the caramel. Cut each mango slice in half crosswise. Cut into a 2-inch (5-cm) round. Place 1 round on top of each slice of pineapple. Bake in the preheated oven for 30 minutes.

■ Remove from the oven and top each ramekin or cup with a puff pastry circle. Bake for 10 minutes, or the pastry is golden brown and puffed. Remove from the oven and immediately flip the ramekins or cups over onto 4 serving plates. Serve immediately, with a puddle of raspberry coulis and a scoop of fruit sorbet, if desired. *Makes 4 individual tarts*

JOHANNES VERMEER *Young Woman with a Water Pitcher* c. 1660–1667

THE METROPOLITAN MUSEUM OF ART
NEW YORK, NEW YORK

All these great works of art are great teachers . . . They teach you about humanity, just like all great literature . . . and they teach you how to uplift yourself rather than bring yourself down. They teach you about life and what a precious, precious thing it is to be a human being.

—Tony Bennett

The Metropolitan Museum of Art (the Met), one of the world's greatest museums, has the largest collection of art in the Western Hemisphere. With holdings of more than two million works spanning five thousand years of world culture, the Met can send museum-goers to Egypt, Renaissance Italy, and nineteenth-century France, all in one afternoon. And given the breadth of each of the many museums within a museum that make up the Met, there is unparalleled opportunity for in-depth study and a myriad of reasons for repeated visits.

The Met was founded in 1870 by a group of businessmen, financiers, and leading artists and thinkers who wanted to bring art and art education to the American people. In 1880, the museum moved to its present location, a massive Gothic Revival–style building on the edge of Central Park. The museum has undergone numerous expansions since its inception, and currently spans four blocks (from Eightieth to Eighty-fourth Streets) along Fifth Avenue. The Met's magnificent facade and entrance were completed in 1926.

The Metropolitan's collection of European paintings includes important works by masters such as Vermeer, Rembrandt, Botticelli, Degas, and Monet. The American Wing is renowned for its comprehensive collection of American paintings, sculpture, and decorative arts, including twenty-four period rooms that offer views of American history and domestic life. The most comprehensive collection of Egyptian art outside of Cairo is a favorite with museum visitors, as are the collections of arms and armor, costumes, musical instruments, photography, and medieval and Renaissance art.

Concerts & Lectures at the Met, the oldest continuously presented major concert series in New York, has a vital presence in the city's cultural community. The series offers concerts by renowned artists, concerts with commentary, thematic programs, exhibition-related concerts, and lectures by celebrity speakers, distinguished

MENU

MUSEUM RESTAURANT

■

*Tuscan White Bean Soup
with Porcini and Truffles*

*Speck and Gorgonzola
Quiche*

*Cheesecake with
Mango and Raspberry
Coulis*

scholars, and museum curators. Activities such as walking tours, family events, workshops, and gallery talks are free to museum visitors, and thousands of school classes visit the museum annually. Visiting classes receive family passes that encourage students to return at no cost with their families. Although less visible, the Met's work in the field of art history, which provides numerous internships, grants, and resources to students and scholars, is as important as the more public outreach programs.

There are a variety of dining options at the Met, including two cafés, a cafeteria, and the Great Hall Balcony Bar, where visitors can enjoy drinks, appetizers, and classical music on Friday and Saturday evenings. A stroll through the museum's Greek and Roman galleries leads to The Museum Restaurant. Delicious entrées and desserts, such as the ones that follow, are served at lunch, for Sunday brunch, and on Friday and Saturday evenings in a grand court surrounded by massive columns.

EDWARD STEICHEN *The Flatiron* 1904

ANTONIO STRADIVARI *Violin* 1693

TUSCAN WHITE BEAN SOUP
WITH PORCINI AND TRUFFLES

Comforting and richly flavorful, this soup makes a warming first course and can be a light meal in itself when served with crusty bread and a tossed green salad.

1¹/2 cups (10¹/2 oz/330 g) dried small white beans

¹/2 ounce (15 g) dried porcini mushrooms

2 tablespoons olive oil

1 onion, diced

1 garlic clove, minced

6 cups (48 fl oz/1.5 l) chicken stock (see Basics) or canned low-salt chicken broth

Leaves from 1 sprig fresh thyme, minced

1 small bay leaf

Salt and freshly ground pepper to taste

¹/8 ounce (3.5 g) sliced truffles,* or truffle oil for drizzling

■ Soak the beans overnight in water to cover by 2 inches (5 cm); drain. Alternatively, put the beans in a large saucepan and add water to cover. Bring to a boil and cook for 2 minutes. Remove from heat, cover, and let stand for 1 hour; drain.

■ In a small bowl, soak the porcini in hot water to cover for 30 minutes. Drain and chop the porcini, reserving the soaking liquid.

■ In a large, heavy saucepan over low heat, heat the olive oil and cook the onion and garlic, stirring frequently, for 10 to 15 minutes, or until golden. Add the porcini and their liquid, stirring to scrape up any browned bits from the bottom of the pan. Increase heat to high and cook until the liquid has almost evaporated. Add the beans, stock or broth, thyme, and bay leaf. Bring to a boil, reduce heat to low, and simmer until the beans are tender, about 1¹/2 hours. Remove the bay leaf. Working in batches, transfer the soup to a blender or food processor and purée. If the soup is too thick, add more stock or broth. Season with salt and pepper. Ladle the soup into bowls. Garnish with truffles or a drizzle of truffle oil and serve immediately. *Makes 4 to 6 servings*

* Truffles may be ordered by mail from Urbani Truffles USA, (800) 281-2330.

SPECK AND GORGONZOLA QUICHE

This quiche Lorraine gone Italian makes a perfect brunch or luncheon entrée. If you prefer, substitute bacon and shredded Swiss cheese for the speck and Gorgonzola.

1 tablespoon olive oil

2 ounces (60 g) cipollini or small white onions, sliced

1 cup (8 fl oz/250 ml) heavy cream

2 eggs

2 egg yolks

9-inch (23-cm) partially baked tart shell (see Basics)

1/2 cup (3 oz/90 g) crumbled Gorgonzola cheese

4 ounces (125 g) speck* or prosciutto, chopped

6 fresh sage leaves, minced

Salt and freshly ground pepper to taste

■ Preheat the oven to 325°F (165°C). In a small frying pan over medium heat, heat the olive oil and sauté the onions for 3 minutes, or until translucent. Remove from heat and let cool. In a medium bowl, whisk the cream, eggs, and egg yolks together.

■ Sprinkle the gorgonzola, onions, speck or prosciutto, sage, salt, and pepper into the tart shell. Add the cream mixture. Bake in the preheated oven for 25 minutes, or until puffed and set. Remove from the oven and let cool to room temperature on a wire rack. *Makes 6 to 8 servings*

* Speck is a fatty ham that is smoked with herbs and spices, then air-dried. It comes from the Tyrol, near the Swiss-Italian border, and is available from Italian foods stores and some specialty foods markets.

PIERRE-AUGUST RENOIR *Two Young Girls at the Piano* 1892

CHEESECAKE WITH MANGO AND RASPBERRY COULIS

Prepare this luscious cheesecake at least 4 hours before serving. It tastes even better when prepared a day in advance.

1¹/₂ pounds (750 g) cream cheese at
   room temperature
¹/₂ cup (4 oz/125 g) sugar
3 egg yolks
1 egg
1 cup (8 fl oz/250 ml) heavy cream
¹/₂ teaspoon vanilla extract

GARNISH
Mango Coulis (recipe follows)
Raspberry Coulis (recipe follows)

■ Preheat the oven to 275°F (135°C). Butter a 8¹/₂-inch (21.5-cm) round springform pan and sprinkle lightly with sugar. To prevent leaks, set the pan on 2 squares of aluminum foil and mold the foil up around the sides.

■ In the bowl of a heavy-duty electric mixer, beat the cream cheese and sugar until smooth. With the machine running, add the egg yolks and eggs one at a time, using a spatula to scrape down the sides of bowl as needed. Add the cream and vanilla and beat until perfectly smooth. Pour the batter into the prepared pan and transfer to a large baking dish. Add water to the baking dish to come two-thirds of the way up the sides of the pan. Bake in the preheated oven for 1¹/₂ hours, or until a skewer inserted in the middle comes out clean. Transfer the pan from the oven to a wire rack. Using a knife, loosen the cake from the sides of the pan. Let cool to room temperature, about 30 minutes, then remove the sides. Cover and refrigerate for at least 4 hours before serving. (Can be made up to 4 days ahead. Cover loosely and keep refrigerated.)

■ To serve, slice the cheesecake into wedges. Decorate each plate with a little mango and raspberry coulis and arrange a cheesecake wedge in the center. *Makes 8 to 10 servings*

(continued)

Mango Coulis

1 ripe mango, peeled and cut from the pit
$^1/_4$ cup (2 oz/60 g) sugar
$^1/_4$ cup (2 fl oz/60 ml) hot water

■ In a blender or food processor, combine all the ingredients and purée. Strain the coulis through a fine-mesh sieve into a bowl, pressing it through with the back of a large spoon. *Makes about 1 cup (8 fl oz/250 ml)*

Raspberry Coulis

2 cups (8 oz/250 g) fresh raspberries
$^1/_4$ cup (2 oz/60 g) sugar
$^1/_4$ cup (2 fl oz/60 ml) hot water

■ In a blender or food processor, combine all the ingredients and purée. Strain through a fine-mesh sieve into a bowl, pressing it through with the back of a large spoon. *Makes about 1 cup (8 fl oz/250 ml)*

THE METROPOLITAN MUSEUM OF ART

PAUL CÉZANNE *Still Life with Apples and a Pot of Primroses* early 1890s

JOHN SINGER SARGENT *Mrs. Fiske Warren (Gretchen Osgood) and Her Daughter Rachel* 1903

MUSEUM OF FINE ARTS, BOSTON

BOSTON, MASSACHUSETTS

The treasures at the Museum of Fine Arts, Boston are truly inspiring—evoking the creative artist in all of us. With works ranging from Impressionist masterpieces to ancient Egyptian sculpture, the MFA offers a place of beauty and tranquility for visitors around the world, presenting art in innovative ways that deepen experience. —Jacques Pépin

The Museum of Fine Arts, Boston (MFA), one of the greatest encyclopedic museums in the world, is visited by more than one million people annually. In 1870, the Massachusetts legislature passed an act establishing a board of trustees "for the purpose of erecting a museum for the preservation and exhibition of works of art," and in 1876 the Museum of Fine Arts moved to its current home, a neoclassical granite structure on Huntington Avenue. The museum's West Wing, designed by the always inspiring architect I. M. Pei, was added in 1981. In 2002, the MFA unveiled a major plan for renovation developed by Pritzker Prize–winning architect Norman Foster. His new plan goes back to the museum's 1909 master plan and promises that the museum will be the first great Boston public building of the twenty-first century.

The MFA's outstanding collection of European paintings includes the largest grouping of Claude Monet paintings outside France. Visitors also enjoy the superb collection of American art, including Paul Revere's silver Liberty Bowl and portraits by John Singleton Copley and Gilbert Stuart. The MFA's distinguished collection of Egyptian art dates from 1905, when the museum joined Harvard University in an archaeological expedition at the base of the Great Pyramids at Giza. The MFA holdings in Asian art, particularly the art of Japan, are world renowned.

In addition to art, lectures, films, musical performances, and activities for families, museum-goers can enjoy three enchanting gardens: a European garden dating back to 1928; a courtyard used for outdoor concerts and alfresco dining; and the MFA's Japanese Garden, Tenshin-en, or "The Garden in the Heart of Heaven." The MFA has a sister museum in Nagoya, Japan, as well as a partnership with the National Center of Afro-American Artists. Also connected to the museum is the acclaimed School of the Museum of Fine Arts.

The MFA recognizes that, as inspiring as the masterpieces in its galleries are, people can't live on fine art alone. There are three restaurants within the museum. The Fraser Garden Court Terrace restaurant offers innovative, Mediterranean-inspired cuisine for lunch and dinner. Guests linger in a casual, art-filled room that looks out through a stunning glass wall to a serene outdoor courtyard. The Galleria Café offers sidewalk-café-style dining in the West Wing, and snacks and casual meals are available in the family-friendly Courtyard Café, with outdoor seating in Calderwood Courtyard when weather permits. The following recipes were created by chef Benjamin Cevelo and pastry chef Kristen Eycleshymer of Fraser Garden Court Terrace.

CYRUS E. DALLIN *The Appeal to the Great Spirit* 1909

HILAIRE GERMAIN EDGAR DEGAS
Degas' Father Listening to Lorenzo Pangano Playing the Guitar c. 1869–1872

WILLIAM MICHAEL HARNETT *Still Life with Violin* 1885

NEW ENGLAND CLAM CHOWDER

Serve this beloved white chowder as a starter, or with a green salad as the main course for an informal lunch or family dinner. For a more flavorful soup, make the chowder the day before you plan to serve it so the flavors have a chance to blend.

8 slices bacon, diced
2 onions, diced
2 celery stalks, diced
1 large carrot, peeled and diced
1/2 cup (4 fl oz/125 ml) dry white wine
1 tablespoon minced fresh thyme
2 bay leaves
Salt and freshly ground pepper to taste
2 red or white potatoes, peeled and
    neatly diced
8 cups (64 fl oz/2 l) fish stock (see
    Basics), clam juice, or canned low-
    salt chicken broth, or more as needed
1 cup (8 fl oz/250 ml) heavy cream

1 pound (500 g) clams, scrubbed
    (discard any that are gaping and
    do not close when tapped)
8 ounces (250 g) boneless, skinless fish
    fillets such as cod, hake, haddock,
    monkfish, halibut, or sea bass, cut
    into 2-inch (5-cm) chunks
1 pound (500 g) shrimp, shelled and
    deveined
8 ounces (250 g) sea scallops
Juice of 1 lemon
6 drops Tabasco sauce, or to taste
1 tablespoon *each* minced fresh
    flat-leaf parsley and chives

■ In a large, heavy soup pot over medium heat, fry the bacon for about 7 minutes, or until slightly crisp. Using a slotted spoon, transfer to paper towels to drain. Add the onions, celery, and carrot and sauté for 15 to 20 minutes, or until the vegetables are tender but not browned. Stir in the wine, thyme, bay leaves, salt, and pepper. Cook for 3 minutes. Add the potatoes and pour in enough fish stock, clam juice, or chicken broth to cover by 1 inch (2.5 cm). Raise heat to high and bring to a boil. Reduce heat to low and simmer for 20 minutes, or until the potatoes are tender. Transfer 2 cups (16 fl oz/500 ml) of the mixture to a blender or food processor and purée. Return to the pot and bring to a simmer.

■ Meanwhile, in a small, heavy saucepan, simmer the cream over medium-low heat until reduced by half. Remove cream from heat and set aside.

■ Add the clams, fish chunks, shrimp, and scallops to the soup pot. Cover and cook until the clams have opened; discard any that do not open. Stir in the lemon juice, Tabasco, and reduced cream. Ladle the chowder into warmed bowls, garnish with parsley and chives, and serve piping hot. *Makes 8 to 10 servings*

TWO-BEAN AND ROASTED-BEET SALAD

Brilliant colors and vibrant flavors combine in this superb salad.

2 ruby or Chioggia* beets
Olive oil for coating
8 ounces (250 g) wax beans, trimmed
8 ounces (250 g) green beans,
  trimmed

Citrus Vinaigrette (recipe follows)
4 paper-thin slices prosciutto di Parma
3/4 cup (4 oz/125 g) crumbled fresh
  white goat cheese

- Preheat the oven to 450°F (230°C). Trim the beets, leaving 1 inch (2.5 cm) of stem, and scub them well; do not peel. Place them in a baking dish and coat them with olive oil. Roast in the preheated oven for 1 to 1½ hours, or until tender. Let cool, then peel and slice thinly.
- Cook the wax beans and green beans in a large pot of salted boiling water for 5 to 7 minutes, or until crisp-tender. Drain, rinse under cold water, and drain again. In a large bowl, toss the beans with the citrus vinaigrette.
- To serve, place a mound of beets in the center of each of 4 plates and top each mound with a slice of prosciutto. Arrange the beans around the prosciutto and sprinkle with the goat cheese. *Makes 4 to 6 servings*

* Chioggia beets have circular red and white stripes; look for them in specialty produce markets.

CITRUS VINAIGRETTE

2 tablespoons fresh lemon juice
1/2 garlic clove, minced
1 small shallot, minced
2 tablespoons Champagne or balsamic
  vinegar

1 cup (8 fl oz/250 ml) extra-virgin
  olive oil
1 teaspoon minced fresh thyme
1 teaspoon honey
Salt and freshly ground pepper to taste

- In a medium bowl, whisk all the ingredients together. *Makes about 1¼ cups (10 fl oz/180 ml)*

PROSCIUTTO-WRAPPED CHICKEN WITH TOASTED-ALMOND PESTO

The bright, fresh flavor of this pesto makes a delightful accent for chicken.

4 boneless chicken breast halves, preferably free-range

Salt and freshly ground pepper to taste

2 tablespoons olive oil

4 paper-thin slices prosciutto di Parma

6 fresh artichoke hearts, (see Basics), quartered lengthwise

1 lemon

TOASTED-ALMOND PESTO

8 tablespoons (2 oz/60 g) slivered almonds, toasted (see Basics)

1 small bunch fresh basil, stemmed, washed, and dried

2 garlic cloves

1 small handful arugula leaves

Juice of 1 lemon

$^{1}/_{2}$ cup (4 fl oz/125 ml) extra-virgin olive oil

$^{1}/_{4}$ cup (1 oz/30 g) grated Parmesan cheese

2 tomatoes, thinly sliced

■ Rinse the chicken breasts and pat them dry; season with salt and pepper. In a large frying pan over medium heat, heat the olive oil and sauté the chicken for about 5 minutes on each side, or until golden brown. Transfer to a plate and let cool. Wrap each breast with a slice of prosciutto and transfer to a baking dish. Bake in the preheated oven for 10 minutes, or until the juices run clear when the chicken is pierced at the thickest point.

■ Meanwhile, make the pesto: In a blender or food processor, combine 6 table-spoons of the almonds, the basil, garlic, arugula, and lemon juice. Purée until smooth. With the machine running, gradually add the olive oil to make an emulsified sauce. Stir in the Parmesan cheese.

■ To serve, place 2 or 3 tomato slices in the center of each of 4 plates and season with salt and pepper. Arrange 4 artichoke quarters around each serving of tomatoes. Arrange the chicken breasts over the tomatoes. Drizzle with the pesto and sprinkle with the remaining almonds. *Makes 4 servings*

HENRI FANTIN-LATOUR *Flowers and Fruit on a Table* 1865

Maple Crème Brûlée

Delicately flavored with maple, this silky custard has a crisp sugar topping.

2 cups (16 fl oz/500 ml) half-and-half
1/2 vanilla bean, split lengthwise, or
  1/2 teaspoon vanilla extract
5 egg yolks

1/2 cup (4 oz/125 g) sugar, plus
  4 tablespoons for topping
2 teaspoons pure maple extract

- Preheat the oven to 325°F (165°C). In a saucepan over medium heat, combine the half-and-half and the vanilla bean, if using. Heat until bubbles form around the edges of the pan. Remove from heat, cover, and set aside to steep for 15 minutes. Remove the bean and scrape the seeds back into the half-and-half.
- In a medium bowl, beat the egg yolks and 1/2 cup (4 oz/125 g) sugar together until pale. Gradually stir the cream mixture into the egg yolk mixture. Stir in the maple extract and the vanilla extract, if using.
- Place four 3-inch (7-cm) ramekins in a baking pan and pour the custard into the ramekins. Add hot water to the baking pan to come halfway up the sides of the ramekins. Bake in the preheated oven for 30 to 35 minutes, or until the mixture is just set but still trembling in the center. Let cool. Refrigerate for at least 3 hours.
- Just before serving, preheat the broiler. Place 1 tablespoon sugar in a small fine-mesh sieve and push the sugar through with the back of a spoon to evenly layer the top of a custard. Repeat with the remaining custards. Place the custards on a baking sheet under the broiler about 2 inches from the heat source and broil until the sugar is melted and crisp, 1 to 2 minutes; be careful not to burn. Let cool for a few minutes and serve. *Makes 4 custards*

PAUL REVERE II *Coffee Pot* c. 1791

CLAUDE MONET *Water Lilies (Nymphéas)* 1907

THE MUSEUM OF FINE ARTS, HOUSTON
HOUSTON, TEXAS

Houston epitomizes the vibrant entrepreneurial energy and generous spirit that is associated with Texans. The Museum of Fine Arts Houston plays a vital role reflecting that spirit. To Houston's diversified communities our museum offers the best of the best to anyone.

—Lynn Wyatt, Founding Chairperson of the
Film Committee, Museum of Fine Arts, Houston

Founded in 1900 as the Public School Art League, the Museum of Fine Arts, Houston (MFAH) was the first art museum established in Texas. Today, visitors enjoy the largest encyclopedic art collection in the Southwestern United States. The original Beaux-Arts museum building was built in 1924 and transformed into a major landmark of modern architecture by Bauhaus architect Mies van der Rohe, whose additions were completed in 1958 and 1974. The Houston museum more than doubled its exhibition space in March 2000 by opening the Audrey Jones Beck Building. Designed by Spanish architect Rafael Moneo, the Beck Building is noted for its classically proportioned galleries, with natural light filtered through innovative rooftop lanterns and skylights. A large sculpture garden designed by Isamu Noguchi is also part of the MFAH campus. An oasis of grass, trees, and fountains, the garden displays important nineteenth- and twentieth-century sculptures by Auguste Rodin, Henri Matisse, Alberto Giacometti, Frank Stella, and others.

When MFAH first opened, its collection included only fifty artworks. Today the museum has more than forty thousand works, many of them gifts from a series of devoted donors. In 1941, for instance, Percy Straus and Edith Abraham gave eighty-two works from their brilliant collection of Old Masters. The museum's Impressionist and Post-Impressionist collection was largely donated by Audrey Jones Beck, who visited Paris for the first time at the age of sixteen and fell in love with the works of artists such as Pissarro, Renoir, and Van Gogh. Museum visitors are especially fond of the dazzling Glassell Collection of African Gold, one of the most comprehensive collections of nineteenth- and twentieth-century African gold objects in the world. MFAH's commitment to becoming a primary showcase for Latin American art in the United States is evident in many special exhibitions focusing on artists from Mexico, Central America, and South America.

Every Sunday is family day at the Museum of Fine Arts, Houston. Children and their parents may participate in a variety of drop-in art activities including workshops, storytelling, and postcard treasure hunts through the collections. Artful Thursdays are informal evenings for adults to enjoy monthly lectures, walking tours, art making workshops, and performances. The museum also sponsors a lively film program with classics and new screenings.

The following recipes are from Cafe Express, which is located on the lower level of the Beck building. The café offers pastas, salads, sandwiches, soups, and desserts in a casual, art-filled setting looking out onto a sunken garden and terraced waterfall. The café is especially popular on the first Friday of every month when visitors can enjoy dinner, drinks, and music after touring the museum. Executive chef is Robert Del Grande, of the Schiller Del Grande Restaurant Group and chef/owner of Cafe Annie, Houston's popular fine dining restaurant.

CRISTOFORO MUNARI *Still Life with Musical Instruments* c. 1710–1715

CAMILLE COROT *Orpheus Leading Eurydice from the Underworld* 1861

Shrimp Campeche with Salsa

Prepare the salsa a few hours ahead and add the shrimp and avocados just before serving.

1 yellow bell pepper
1 red bell pepper
Olive oil for coating
4 Roma (plum) tomatoes, or
  2 salad tomatoes
6 tomatillos,* husked and rinsed
4 garlic cloves
1 small white onion, quartered
1 to 2 jalapeno chilies, seeded
1 cup (1 oz/30 g) chopped fresh cilantro
  leaves, plus 1 cilantro sprig for garnish

$^1/_2$ cup (4 fl oz/125 ml) tomato juice
Salt to taste
1 tablespoon fresh lime juice or
  to taste
1 teaspoon maple syrup or packed
  brown sugar
2 Haas avocados, peeled, pitted, and
  finely diced
1 pound (500 g) cooked shrimp, diced
Tortilla chips (see Basics) or toasted
  baguette slices for serving

■ Preheat the broiler. Coat the bell peppers with olive oil. Line a broiler tray with aluminum foil and arrange the tomatoes, tomatillos, garlic cloves, onion, jalapenos, and bell peppers, skin side up, in a single layer.

■ Broil the vegetables for 5 to 10 minutes, or until the bell peppers and tomatillos are charred and blistered. Turn all the ingredients over and broil 5 to 10 minutes longer, or until charred on the other side. Remove the vegetables from the oven and transfer the bell peppers and tomatillos to a paper or plastic bag, close it, and let the peppers and tomatillos cool for 10 minutes. Remove the vegetables from the bag and peel off their skins with your fingers or a small, sharp knife. Halve the bell peppers and remove the stem and seeds.

■ Transfer all the broiled ingredients to a blender or food processor. Add the chopped cilantro, the tomato juice, salt, lime juice, and maple syrup or brown sugar, if using. Process until coarsely puréed. Transfer the salsa to a serving bowl and refrigerate for at least 2 hours or up to 6 hours.

■ Just before serving, stir the avocados and shrimp into the salsa and mix well. Garnish with a cilantro sprig and serve with tortilla chips or toasted baguette slices. *Makes 4 servings*

* Tomatillos resemble small green tomatoes with a thin husk. They are available in the produce section of many supermarkets and in Latino markets.

MUSEUM OF FINE ARTS, HOUSTON

SPICY SHRIMP AND AVOCADO SALAD

A crunchy, smoky, brightly colored salad with many layers of flavor.

8 romaine lettuce leaves, chopped into bite-sized pieces

8 ounces (250 g) jicama, (about 2 cups) cut into matchsticks

8 cherry tomatoes, stemmed and halved

2 avocados, peeled, pitted, and diced

24 medium shrimp, cooked, shelled and deveined

$^1/_2$ cup (4 fl oz/125 ml) Chipotle Sauce (recipe follows)

$^1/_4$ cup (2 fl oz/60 ml) Honey-Mustard Ranch Dressing (recipe follows)

4 handfuls mixed baby salad greens

Grated Parmesan cheese for sprinkling

2 slices bacon, cooked and crumbled

■ In a large bowl, combine the romaine lettuce, jicama, tomatoes, avocados, and shrimp. Toss gently with the chipotle sauce and ranch dressing until well mixed.

■ To serve, divide the romaine mixture among 4 large shallow bowls. Sprinkle each serving with baby salad greens, Parmesan cheese, and bacon. *Makes 4 servings*

CHIPOTLE SAUCE

2 tablespoons finely chopped onion

1 garlic clove

2 Roma (plum) tomatoes

2 canned chipotles en adobo, drained

$^1/_2$ teaspoon salt

1 teaspoon maple syrup

1 teaspoon fresh lime juice

2 tablespoons minced fresh cilantro

■ Preheat the oven to 450°F (230°C). On a baking sheet, evenly spread out the onion and garlic clove and top with the tomatoes. Roast in the preheated oven for 30 minutes. Remove from the oven and let cool slightly. Transfer to a blender or food processor and add the chipotles, salt, maple syrup, and lime juice. Process for 15 seconds, or just until the sauce begins to break down; do not overprocess. Stir in the cilantro and refrigerate for up to 3 days. *Makes about 1 cup (8 fl oz/250 ml)*

WILLEM CLAESZ HEDA *Banquet Piece with Ham* 1656

HONEY MUSTARD RANCH DRESSING

$^1/_4$ cup (2 fl oz/60 ml) buttermilk

$^1/_4$ cup (2 fl oz/60 ml) heavy cream

$^1/_4$ cup (2 oz/60 g) mayonnaise

$^1/_4$ cup (2 oz/60 g) Dijon mustard

$^1/_4$ cup (3 oz/90g) honey

$^1/_2$ teaspoon Tabasco sauce

1 tablespoon fresh lime juice

$^1/_2$ teaspoon minced fresh rosemary

Salt and freshly ground pepper

to taste

■ In a medium bowl, combine all the ingredients. Whisk until blended.
Makes about 1 cup (8 fl oz/250 ml)

TEXAS PECAN PIE

A beloved Southern dessert.

PIE DOUGH
1 cup (5 oz/155 g) all-purpose flour
2 teaspoons sugar
$^1/_4$ teaspoon salt
$^1/_2$ cup (4 oz/125 g) cold butter, cut
  into small pieces
$^1/_4$ cup (2 fl oz/60 ml) chilled water

FILLING
4 eggs
2 egg yolks
1 tablespoon vanilla extract
1 cup (7 oz/220 g) packed brown sugar
$^1/_4$ teaspoon salt
2 tablespoons butter, melted
$1^1/_2$ cups (15 oz/470 g) light corn syrup
$1^1/_2$ cups (6 oz/185 g) pecan pieces

■ To make the pie dough: In a food processor, combine the flour, sugar, salt, and butter and process until crumbly. Pour in the water and process until the dough just forms a ball. Or, in a medium bowl, combine the flour, sugar, salt, and butter. Using a pastry cutter or 2 knives, cut in the butter until the mixture resembles coarse crumbs. Gradually stir in the water with a fork and stir until the dough comes together to form a ball.

■ On a lightly floured surface, knead the dough briefly and roll it out to a round 10-inches (25-cm) in diameter. Fit the dough into a 9-inch (23-cm) pie plate and form a decorative crust. Refrigerate for 30 minutes.

■ Preheat the oven to 375°F (190°C). To make the filling: In a medium bowl, whisk the eggs and egg yolks together. Stir in the vanilla, brown sugar, salt, and melted butter. Pour in the corn syrup and mix well.

■ Sprinkle the pecans evenly in the bottom of the pie shell and pour in the filling. Transfer the pie to a baking sheet and bake in the preheated oven for 15 minutes. Reduce the heat to 300°F (150°C) and bake for 50 to 60 minutes, or until the center puffs slightly and the crust is golden brown. Remove from the oven and let cool slightly or completely. *Makes one 9-inch pie*

MUSEUM OF FINE ARTS, HOUSTON

PABLO PICASSO *Three Musicians* Fontainebleau, summer 1921

THE MUSEUM OF MODERN ART
NEW YORK, NEW YORK

When Leonard and I were dating, we spent many happy hours at the MoMA. In spite of the fact that he's the Chairman of the Whitney Museum of American Art, when we want to read the pulse of world art today, we always enjoy the shows at the MoMA—we feel as if we're still dating.

—Evelyn Lauder

In 1929, three patrons of the arts—Lillie P. Bliss, Mary Quinn Sullivan, and Abby Aldrich Rockefeller—decided to open a museum that would make modern and contemporary art available to the public. At that time, the idea of a museum devoted entirely to modern art was innovative, to say the least. Today, more than eighty years later, the Museum of Modern Art (MoMA) has become an integral part of our nation's cultural landscape and a taste-making institution for the world.

Because ideas about modern art are always in flux, MoMA's choices for its permanent collection can be seen as a history of cultural thought during the twentieth century. The museum is currently undergoing a major expansion and renovation to ensure that it will continue to play an important role in the world of twenty-first-century art. There are more than 100,000 paintings, drawings, prints, photographs, sculptures, architectural models, and design objects in the permanent collections. Masterpieces such as Paul Cézanne's *The Bather*, Vincent Van Gogh's *Starry Night*, and Pablo Picasso's *Les Demoiselles d'Avignon* are included in the world's largest collection of modern painting. MoMA was the first museum to create a curatorial department of architecture and design. The design collection includes more than three thousand objects ranging from appliances and furniture to textiles and even a helicopter. The MoMA Film Library was established in 1935 and now includes more than four million film stills and fourteen thousand films. Classic, experimental, and foreign films are shown at the museum free of charge, with the price of admission. MoMA's continuing commitment to exploring the place of technology in modern art is evident in innovative online exhibitions and interactive web projects.

MENU

SETTE MOMA

▪

Riso al Salto

*Spaghetti con
la Salsiccia Italiana*

Ossobuco

*Warm Bittersweet
Chocolate Cakes*

Architect Yoshio Taniguchi's enlarged and renovated MoMA, which will be completed in 2005, includes changes to every aspect of the current building, from facade to gallery spaces. However, the fabled Abby Aldrich Rockefeller Sculpture Garden, one of the most beautiful urban spaces in the world and the model for many sculpture gardens throughout America, will remain at the heart of the building. While the construction is underway, MoMA will move to its new facility in Queens. Los Angeles architect Michael Maltzan has adapted a former Swingline staple factory in Long Island City to house temporary shows and exhibit highlights of the museum's permanent collection.

The following recipes are from Sette MoMA, the museum's contemporary Italian restaurant. Closed during the renovation, Sette MoMA is scheduled to reopen in 2005.

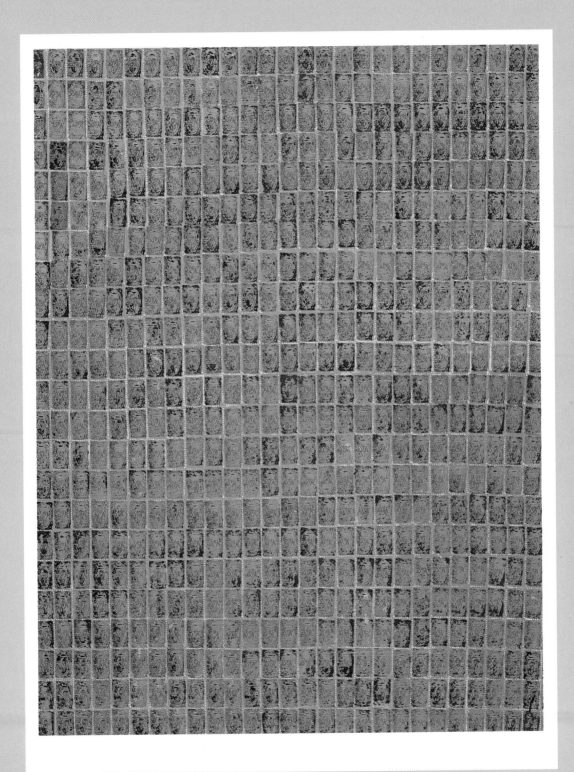

ANDY WARHOL S & H Green Stamps 1962

SPAGHETTI CON LA SALSICCIA ITALIANA
SPAGHETTI WITH ITALIAN SAUSAGE

A simple pasta dish made with sweet Italian sausage, diced zucchini, and Parmesan cheese.

2 tablespoons olive oil

5 garlic cloves, minced

4 sweet Italian sausages, removed from
   casings

4 zucchini, finely diced

1 cup (8 fl oz/250 ml) dry white wine

Salt and freshly ground pepper to taste

1 pound (16 oz/500 g) spaghetti

2 tablespoons butter at room
   temperature

1 cup (4 oz/125 g) grated Parmesan
   cheese

2 tablespoons minced fresh flat-leaf
   parsley

■ In a large frying pan over medium heat, heat the olive oil and sauté the garlic for 3 minutes, or just until golden. Add the sausage meat and sauté, breaking up the pieces, for 3 to 4 minutes, or until browned. Pour off the fat and stir in the zucchini, wine, salt, and pepper. Cook until the wine is reduced by half.

■ Meanwhile, cook the spaghetti in a large pot of salted boiling water for about 10 minutes, or until al dente. Drain and return to the pot or transfer to a warmed large bowl. Add the sauce, butter, and Parmesan cheese and toss until thoroughly mixed. Sprinkle with parsley and serve at once. *Makes 6 servings*

THE MUSEUM OF MODERN ART

RISO AL SALTO
SAFFRON RICE CAKES

Serve these crusty risotto cakes as an appetizer, as a side dish with ossobuco, or for a light meal with a tossed green salad. In Italy, riso al salto *is a traditional after-theater treat following the opera at La Scala.*

2 tablespoons olive oil
1 onion, finely chopped
2 cups (14 oz/440 g) Arborio rice
2 cups (10 oz/315 g) fresh or thawed
  frozen peas
Pinch of saffron threads
8 cups (64 fl oz/2 l) chicken stock
  (see Basics) or canned low-salt
  chicken broth

2^1/$_4$ cups (10 oz/315 g) diced fresh
  mozzarella cheese
^{1}/$_2$ cup (4 oz/125 g) butter at room
  temperature
1 cup (4 oz/125 g) grated Parmesan
  cheese
Salt and freshly ground pepper
  to taste

■ In a large frying pan over medium-low heat, heat the olive oil and sauté the onion until golden, about 5 minutes. Add the rice and stir until opaque, about 2 minutes. Add the peas, saffron, and ^{1}/$_2$ cup (4 fl oz/125 ml) of the stock or broth. Continue adding the stock or broth by ^{1}/$_2$-cup (4-fl oz/125-ml) amounts until all the liquid has been used and the rice is al dente, tender but firm. Remove from heat and stir in the mozzarella, 6 tablespoons (3 oz/90 g) of the butter, the Parmesan cheese, salt, and pepper. Remove from heat. Spread the risotto out on a baking sheet and let cool completely.
■ Form the risotto into 6 pancakes, each ^{1}/$_2$ inch (12 mm) thick. Melt the remaining 2 tablespoons butter in a large frying pan over medium-high heat and cook the pancakes until crisp and browned on both sides. Serve hot.
Makes 6 servings

OSSOBUCO
VEAL SHANKS

The traditional recipe for ossobuco, which literally means "bone with a hole," calls for a garnish of gremolata, a mixture of minced parsley, garlic, and lemon zest. Serve this hearty dish with saffron rice pancakes or risotto.

GREMOLATA
Grated zest of 2 lemons
1 garlic clove, minced
3 heaping tablespoons minced fresh
    flat-leaf parsley

1/2 cup (2 1/2 oz/75 g) all-purpose flour
Salt and freshly ground pepper
    to taste

Six 2-inch (5-cm) sections veal
    hind shank
4 tablespoons (2 oz/60 g) butter
2 tablespoons olive oil
2 red onions, diced
4 celery stalks, chopped
2 garlic cloves, minced
1 1/2 cups (12 fl oz/375 ml) dry white wine
Riso al Salto (page 130) for serving

■ Preheat the oven to 300°F (150°C). Mix all the gremolata ingredients together in a small bowl. Season the flour with salt and pepper and dredge the slices of veal shank in it. Shake off any excess.

■ In a Dutch oven or large, heavy flameproof casserole, melt 2 tablespoons of the butter with the olive oil over medium-high heat and quickly sear the veal on all sides. Using tongs, transfer the meat to paper towels to drain. Pour off the remaining fat.

■ Add the remaining 2 tablespoons butter, melt over medium heat, and sauté the onions and celery until soft but not browned, about 5 minutes. Add the garlic and sauté for 2 or 3 minutes, or until fragrant. Pour in the wine and stir to scrape up any browned bits from the bottom of the pan. Raise heat to high and boil to reduce by half.

■ Return the veal to the casserole, making sure the bones are placed so the marrow won't fall out while cooking. The broth should come up to the top of the veal pieces; add water if it does not. Cover the pot with a round of parchment paper and a lid. Bake in the preheated oven for about 2 hours, or until the meat is very tender.

■ To serve, Divide the veal shanks among 6 plates, pour the sauce over, and sprinkle with the gremolata. Serve with the riso al salto. *Makes 6 servings*

THE MUSEUM OF MODERN ART

WARM BITTERSWEET CHOCOLATE CAKES

Luscious little cakes that capture the essence of deep chocolate flavor.

1 cup (8 oz/250 g) unsalted butter at room temperature

2 cups (16 oz/500 g) packed light brown sugar

4 eggs

2 teaspoons vanilla extract

1 cup (8 fl oz/250 ml) hot water

1$^{1}/_{2}$ cups (7 1/2 oz/235 g) all-purpose flour

$^{1}/_{4}$ teaspoon salt

2 teaspoons baking soda

$^{1}/_{2}$ cup (1$^{1}/_{2}$ oz/45 g) unsweetened cocoa powder

Whipped cream or ice cream for serving

■ Preheat the oven to 325°F (165°C). Butter eight 1-cup (8–fl oz/250 ml) ramekins and dust with flour.

■ Using an electric mixer on high speed, beat the butter and brown sugar together until fluffy. Beat in the eggs, one at a time. Mix in the vanilla and hot water until smooth.

■ In a medium bowl, combine the flour, salt, baking soda, and cocoa. Stir to blend. Gradually stir the flour mixture into the wet ingredients and mix until smooth.

■ Pour the batter into the prepared ramekins. Bake in the preheated oven for 20 minutes, or until a skewer inserted in the center of a cake comes out almost clean. Remove from the oven and let cool slightly. Invert the ramekins onto 6 individual plates. Serve warm, with a dollop of whipped cream or a scoop of ice cream. *Makes 8 individual cakes*

ROBERT RAUSCHENBERG *Factum II* 1957

THE MUSEUM OF MODERN ART

NATIONAL GALLERY OF ART
WASHINGTON, D.C.

Not only does the National Gallery of Art fulfill its role as the treasure house of the cultural heritage of the world, just as the nation does, it is just about the most welcoming of America's institutions—a great meeting ground of artistic passions, at once scholarly, feisty, and funny. —Morley Safer, Correspondent, CBS-TV "60 Minutes"

"Museum visitors are travelers through time and space," according to Earl A. Powell III, director of the National Gallery of Art (NGA). Created for the people of the United States of America by a joint resolution of Congress passed in 1937, the National Gallery allows visitors to move freely through many centuries and geographical regions while viewing some of the world's greatest masterpieces.

The National Gallery is made up of two strikingly different buildings, the East and West Buildings. The West Building, one of the largest marble structures in the world, was a gift to the nation from Andrew W. Mellon, who also contributed the nucleus of the museum's original collections. John Russell Pope, architect of the Jefferson Memorial, designed the West Building. His magnificent rotunda, marble halls, and wide staircases create a classical museum setting.

The museum's spectacular East Building, designed by architect I. M. Pei, rises to the challenge of the trapezoidal plot of land set aside by Congress for the National Gallery's expansion. Opened to the public in 1978, the East Building houses a magnificent collection of twentieth-century art and provides space for special exhibitions. Between the East and West Buildings is an underground concourse with an indoor fountain cascading down one wall, a popular café, and a gift shop.

Perhaps the most important outreach program offered by the National Gallery is the simplest one: Admission to the museum is free at all times. Throughout the year, visitors enjoy films, lectures, and tours of the permanent collection and special exhibitions. The tradition of Sunday-evening concerts at the museum began in the 1940s, and the first annual Andrew W. Mellon Lectures took place in

MARY CASSATT *Afternoon Tea Party* 1890–1891

1952. Tours for schoolchildren, free resources for teachers and schools, and an annual Teacher Institute are among the museum's many educational programs.

Museum-goers can take a break and enjoy sandwiches, salads, soups, and hot entrées at the Cascade Café in the concourse, or stop for drinks and a light meal at the Pavilion Café, which offers panoramic views of the Sculpture Garden with a majestic fountain and contemporary sculpture. At the Garden Café in the West Building, a marble floor and columns, a fountain, and a mass of foliage and flowers create a peaceful setting for an enjoyable lunch. The Garden Café's menu includes traditional American fare and entrées related to current exhibitions.

HENRI MATISSE *Woman with Amphora and Pomegranates* 1953

VINCENT VAN GOGH *The Olive Orchard* 1889

PORTOBELLO BISQUE

A warming first course for a special dinner.

4 portobello mushrooms
2 tablespoons olive oil
5 cups (40 fl oz/1.25 ml) chicken
   stock (see Basics) or canned
   low-salt chicken broth
1 cup (8 oz/250 ml) milk

4 tablespoons (2 oz/60 g) butter at
   room temperature
1/4 cup (2 1/2 oz/75 g) flour
2 1/2 cups (20 fl oz/625 ml) heavy
   cream or half-and-half
Salt and ground white pepper to taste

■ Stem the portobello mushrooms and reserve the caps. Add the stems to a blender or food processor. Process until almost puréed. In a large frying pan over medium heat, heat 1 tablespoon of the olive oil and sauté the ground stems for 5 minutes, or until soft; do not let them brown. Pour in the stock or broth and milk and bring to a boil. Combine the butter and flour and whisk into the soup. Add the cream or half-and-half, salt, and pepper and simmer for about 30 minutes.
■ Meanwhile, finely dice the mushroom caps. In a large frying pan over high heat, heat the remaining 1 tablespoon olive oil and sauté the caps until the liquid has been released and then evaporated and the mushrooms are soft. Season with salt and pepper. Transfer to the soup and simmer for 30 minutes. Serve hot, in shallow soup bowls. *Makes 4 to 6 servings*

MARC CHAGALL *The Hen with the Golden Eggs* 1927/1930

SPINACH-AND-CHEESE-STUFFED CHICKEN BREASTS WITH MARSALA SAUCE

Serve with buttered noodles and fresh asparagus or peas.

4 boneless, skinless chicken breast halves

STUFFING
1 bunch spinach, stemmed
1 cup (4 oz/125 g) shredded smoked Gouda or Gruyère cheese
1 cup (8 oz/250 g) ricotta cheese
1/2 cup (2 oz/60 g) grated Parmesan cheese
2 tablespoons minced fresh basil
2 eggs, beaten
Salt and freshly ground pepper to taste

MARSALA SAUCE
2 tablespoons butter
1 shallot, minced
12 (3 oz/90 g) button mushrooms, sliced
2/3 cup (5 fl oz/160 ml) dry Marsala wine
1/3 cup (3 fl oz/80 ml) chicken stock or canned low-salt chicken broth
1 tablespoon flour
Salt and freshly ground pepper to taste

(continued)

- Preheat the oven to 375°F (190°C). Lightly oil a 9-by-13-inch (23-by-33-cm) baking dish.
- Rinse the spinach leaves well but do not dry them. Put the spinach in a large frying pan, cover, and cook over high heat just until the spinach wilts. Remove from heat and let cool to the touch. Squeeze out all the liquid; chop finely.
- In a medium bowl, combine the spinach, Gouda or Gruyère, ricotta, Parmesan, basil, eggs, salt, and pepper. Stir until well mixed.
- On a work surface, flatten each breast half with the flat end of a meat pounder until thin. Spoon a line of one-fourth of the stuffing down the center of each chicken breast. Fold the chicken over the stuffing and place the breasts, folded side down, in the prepared dish. Season with salt and pepper. Bake in the preheated oven for 25 to 30 minutes, or until an instant-read thermometer inserted in the center of a breast registers 165°F (73°C).
- Meanwhile, make the Marsala sauce: In a medium frying pan, melt 1 tablespoon of the butter over medium-low heat and sauté the shallot for 2 minutes, or until translucent. Add the mushrooms, increase heat to medium-high, and sauté until the mushrooms have released their liquid. Pour in the Marsala and stock or broth. Cook until the liquid is reduced by one-third. Stir in the flour and cook, stirring, for 3 to 4 minutes. Remove from heat and swirl in the remaining 1 tablespoon butter. Season with salt and pepper.
- Arrange a chicken breast on each of 4 plates, spoon the Marsala sauce over, and serve immediately. *Makes 4 servings*

CRÈME CARAMEL

Comfort food of the highest order.

1¹/4 cups (10 oz/315 g) sugar

¹/3 cup (3 fl oz/80 ml) water

4 eggs

1¹/2 cups (12 fl oz/375 ml) milk

1 teaspoon vanilla extract

Fresh raspberries for serving
   (optional)

■ Preheat the oven to 350°F (180°C). In a small, heavy saucepan, combine 1 cup (8 oz/250 g) of the sugar and the water. Bring to a boil over high heat and cook until deep golden brown. Remove from heat and pour the caramel into six 3¹/2-inch (9-cm) ramekins or ovenproof cups. Immediately swirl to coat the bottom and sides of the ramekins.

■ Using an electric mixer, beat the eggs and the remaining ¹/4 cup (2 oz/60 g) sugar for 2 to 3 minutes, or until pale and thick.

■ In a small saucepan over medium heat, heat the milk until almost boiling. Stir in the vanilla. Gradually stir the milk into the eggs; do not whisk, or too much air will get into the mixture. Pour the custard into the prepared ramekins or cups and transfer them to a large baking dish. Fill the dish with warm water to reach three-fourths of the way up the sides of the ramekins or cups.

■ Cover the pan with aluminum foil and bake in the preheated oven for 40 minutes, or until just set. Transfer the custards to a wire rack and let cool. Refrigerate for at least 12 hours before serving. Just before serving, turn each ramekin or cup over onto a plate and gently shake to unmold. Garnish each crème caramel with fresh raspberries, if desired. *Makes 6 servings*

PIERRE BONNARD *Table Set in a Garden* c. 1908

THE PHILADELPHIA MUSEUM OF ART
PHILADELPHIA, PENNSYLVANIA

How lucky I was to grow up in an artistic family in Philadelphia. My brother William H. Moennig III, is the twelfth generation of venerable violinmakers there. My mother and father had glorious voices (Harry Danner was known as the "singing banker") and met while performing with the Choral Arts Society. My brother Harry's beautiful tenor led him to the Metropolitan Opera Workshop. How meaningful it was for me then to climb that magnificent staircase of the Philadelphia Museum of Art for the very first time as a child with my family and experience the power of the treasures that lay within, a power as strong as the one I'd grown to love through music. —Blythe Danner

The Philadelphia Museum of Art (PMA) was established in 1876, when the City of Brotherly Love was the site of the United States Centennial Exposition, the first World's Fair held in America. Today the museum is housed in the imposing Ruth and Raymond G. Perelman Building. Built during the 1920s, it has ten acres of space, and nearly two hundred galleries, making it one of the largest art museums in the United States. When planning the PMA's current home, legendary museum director Fiske Kimball proposed dramatic period galleries—including paintings, sculpture, prints, furniture, and architectural elements—that would create a "walk through time" for museum visitors.

Philadelphia's European collections include Old Masters, Renaissance, Impressionist, Cubist, Dadaist, Surrealist masterpieces, as well as medieval sculpture and stained glass, a thirteenth-century French cloister, and a suite of eighteenth-century French interiors. A fine collection of twentieth-century art includes masters such as Picasso, Brancusi, and Duchamp as well as pop art and contemporary work in many mediums. The PMA has the world's largest collection of works by native son Thomas Eakins. Extensive holdings of Pennsylvania German art and furniture, and silver by early Philadelphia craftsmen are important components of the American collection. Prized objects in the Asian collection include a Japanese ceremonial teahouse, a reconstructed hall from a Chinese Buddhist temple, and a superb collection of Chinese ceramics.

Every Wednesday evening, museum-goers can enjoy an exciting mix of

GEORGES BRAQUE *Violin and Newspaper (Musical Forms)* 1912–1913

films, music performances, tours, demonstrations, and foods related to a special topic. Friday Evenings at the Museum gives Philadelphians a chance to start their weekends with an inspiring stroll through the galleries while enjoying live jazz, followed by supper at the Museum Restaurant. Music in the Galleries, presented in association with the renowned Curtis Institute of Music, is a program of chamber concerts in the galleries. Additionally, a Family & Children's Program includes performances and workshops for parents and children, and there are ongoing art classes for youth.

The award-winning Museum Restaurant offers American regional cuisine to delight the most discerning palate. Chef Tracy Hopkin's popular seasonal menus complement current exhibitions, and his extraordinary Sunday Jazz Brunch includes omelettes, smoked fish, chicken, roasted vegetables, fruits, and baked goods. The Balcony Café and the Museum Cafeteria are available for lighter fare and self-service. The following recipes were created by chef Tracy Hopkins.

THOMAS EAKINS *Antiquated Music: Portrait of Sarah Sagehorn Frishmuth* c. 1900

Pennsylvania German Kitchen c. 1752

BUTTERNUT SQUASH BISQUE

A soothing, pumpkin-colored soup that makes a perfect starter for an autumn or winter dinner party.

4 tablespoons (2 oz/60 g) butter

1 onion, diced

1 butternut squash, peeled, seeded, and cut into 3-inch (7.5) cubes

2 cups (16 fl oz/500 ml) chicken stock (see Basics) or canned low-salt chicken broth

3/4 cup (6 fl oz/180 ml) heavy cream or half-and-half, scalded

2 teaspoons honey

Salt and ground white pepper to taste

■ In a large, heavy pot over low heat, melt the butter and sauté the onion for about 5 minutes, or until soft; do not brown. Add the squash and sauté for 5 minutes. Pour in the stock or broth, increase heat to high, and bring to a boil. Reduce heat to low and simmer for about 20 minutes, or until the squash is easily pierced with a knife.

■ Transfer to a blender or food processor and purée. Return to the pot and stir in the cream, honey, salt, and pepper. Heat through and serve hot. *Makes 6 servings*

SEARED AHI TUNA AND SNOW PEA SALAD WITH WASABI VINAIGRETTE

A light main dish that is as flavorful as it is beautiful.

One 1-inch (2.5-cm) piece fresh ginger, peeled and chopped
^{1}/2 bunch chives, coarsely chopped
1 cup (4 oz/125 g) panko bread crumbs*
1 teaspoon grated lemon zest
1^1/2-pound (750 g) ahi tuna loin
2 tablespoons canola oil, plus more for filming pan

WASABI VINAIGRETTE
1 teaspoon sugar
^{1}/4 cup (2 oz/60 g) white miso**
2 tablespoons rice vinegar
1 tablespoon wasabi powder
1 teaspoon fresh lemon juice
^{1}/4 cup (2 fl oz/60 ml) light soy sauce
1^1/2 tablespoons canola oil

1 pound (16 oz/500 g) snow peas
1 carrot, halved lengthwise and cut into thin diagonal slices
1 ounce (30 g) pea shoots***
3^1/2 ounces (105 g) enoki mushrooms

(continued)

- In a food processor, combine the ginger, chives, bread crumbs, and lemon zest. Process to make a fine powder.
- Brush the tuna with the 2 tablespoons canola oil and dredge in the crumb mixture to coat well.
- Place a large frying pan over medium-high heat, film with canola oil, and heat until almost smoking. Sear the tuna on all sides. Remove from heat and set aside.
- To make the vinaigrette: In a small bowl, stir the sugar, miso, rice vinegar, wasabi, lemon juice, and soy sauce together. Gradually whisk in the canola oil.
- Blanch the snow peas and carrot in a pot of salted boiling water for 1 minute. Drain, rinse under cold water, and drain again.
- In a large bowl, combine the snow peas, carrot, pea shoots, enoki mushrooms, and vinaigrette; toss well. Arrange a mound of salad on each of 4 plates. Thinly slice the tuna and fan the slices over the salad; serve immediately. *Makes 6 servings*

* Panko bread crumbs are packaged dried bread crumbs from Japan, found in specialty foods stores and Asian markets.

** White miso (which is really a pale yellow) is available at some grocery stores, specialty foods stores, and Asian markets.

***Pea shoots are available in some produce stores and Asian markets.

GEORGIA O'KEEFFE *Peach and Glass* 1927

MARCEL DUCHAMP *Chocolate Grinder (No. 1)* 1913

CHOCOLATE SALAMI

Studded with dried cherries, nuts, biscotti, and candied orange peel, this chocolate log resembles a salami in shape. Slice thinly and serve with espresso or hot coffee.

1 cup (4 oz/125 g) sun-dried cherries*

8 ounces (250 g) semisweet chocolate, chopped

4 tablespoons (2 oz/60 g) butter

2 egg yolks, beaten

1/2 cup (4 oz/125 g) sugar

1/2 cup (2 oz/60 g) slivered almonds

1/2 cup (2 oz/60 g) pistachios, finely chopped

6 plain biscotti, crushed

2 tablespoons chopped candied orange peel

2 tablespoons Grand Marnier

Raspberry Coulis for serving (page 98)

Fresh raspberries for garnish (optional)

■ Put the cherries in a small bowl and add boiling water to barely cover. Let soak for 30 minutes; drain.

■ In a heavy, medium saucepan, combine the chocolate and butter and melt over low heat. Stir in all the remaining ingredients except the raspberry coulis and optional raspberries. Remove from heat and let cool completely. Transfer to a sheet of waxed paper or parchment paper and shape into a 12-inch (30-cm) sausage. Refrigerate for at least 4 hours, or until firm.

■ To serve, thinly slice the log and fan 3 slices in the center of each plate. Drizzle with raspberry coulis and garnish with fresh raspberries, if desired. *Makes 4 to 6 servings*

* Dried cherries are available at specialty foods stores or from Cherry Republic, (800) 206-6949.

PABLO PICASSO *Nature morte "La Cafetière"* (Still Life "The Coffee Pot") 1944

SAN FRANCISCO MUSEUM OF MODERN ART
SAN FRANCISCO, CALIFORNIA

The San Francisco Museum of Modern Art reflects the vibrant role that art plays in the culture and diversity of San Francisco. The museum building is striking in its modernist design and complements the world-class artwork contained within. From paintings to sculptures, photography to new media, the San Francisco Museum of Modern Art extends and challenges visitors' conceptions of art and creativity. As a part of the Yerba Buena Gardens, the Museum is truly an oasis for art enlightenment in the center of the urban landscape, a treasure for the curious and a centerpiece of the cultural soul of San Francisco.

— Willie Lewis Brown, Jr., Mayor of San Francisco

The San Francisco Museum of Modern Art (SFMOMA) is housed in a Mario Botta–designed building that is itself a work of art. According to the Swiss architect, a museum is a "place of common encounter and confrontation . . . to challenge the hopes and contradictions of our times." His museum design is dramatic: a soaring central atrium greets visitors as they enter, and flying bridges, balconies, and generous open spaces let museum-goers experience the space from various viewpoints.

Founded in 1935, SFMOMA was the first museum on the West Coast devoted solely to twentieth century art. The permanent collection includes over twenty thousand works and is especially noted for Abstract Expressionist paintings by American artists such as Jackson Pollock and Richard Diebenkorn. Other strengths include German Expressionism; Fauvism, particularly the works of Henri Matisse; a growing collection of works by Paul Klee; Mexican painting; and art of the San Francisco Bay Area. The SFMOMA has always recognized photography as an important modern art form. With support and advice from photographer Ansel Adams, early curators began acquisitions that are now part of one of the world's most distinguished photography collections. Because the Bay Area is a center for new technologies, SFMOMA was one of the first museums in the United States to establish a permanent media arts department featuring film, video, and other electronic and time-based art.

MENU

CAFFÈ MUSEO

■

Fava Bean Purée

Fig and Gorgonzola Tart

Semolina Gnocchi

*Deep-Dish Apple and
Rhubarb Crisp*

The SFMOMA's varied outreach programs include lectures and symposiums, Art and Conversation events, and programs designed for children, teenagers, and families. In addition, the Louise Sloss Ackerman Fine Arts Library opens to the public by appointment and offers access to over fifty thousand monographs, serials, and exhibition catalogs, as well as artists' books and individual artists' files.

Visitors to SFMOMA can enjoy breakfast, lunch, and light snacks at the award-winning Caffè Museo. Executive chef Gordon Drysdale's seasonal menu focuses on fresh, flavorful selections with country Mediterranean influences. The popular Caffè's stylish black, chrome, and natural maple interior includes furnishings by architect Mario Botta. In fine weather, visitors enjoy lunch or an afternoon pizza or espresso at outdoor tables located near the museum entrance while watching a stream of passersby.

EDWARD WESTON *Cabbage Leaf* 1931

160

FAVA BEAN PURÉE

Serve this flavorful starter in late spring or early summer, when fava beans are in season. Peeling fava beans is a mindless task, but it is definitely worth the effort. Once the beans are peeled, this dish can be prepared quickly.

2 pounds (1 kg) fava beans, shelled
  (about 2 cups)
2 tablespoons extra-virgin olive oil
1 garlic clove, smashed

1 small sprig fresh rosemary
Salt and freshly ground pepper to taste
Grilled or toasted country bread slices
  for serving

■ Cook the fava beans in a large pot of salted boiling water for 1 minute. Drain and run under cold water. Using your fingernails, pinch off a small piece of the skin and slip out the beans.

■ In a medium saucepan over medium-low heat, heat the olive oil. Add the fava beans, garlic, and rosemary. Cook until the beans can be easily mashed with the back of a spoon. Remove the rosemary sprig. Transfer the bean mixture to a blender or food processor and purée. Season with salt and pepper. Serve warm, with grilled or toasted bread for spreading. *Makes 4 servings*

FIG AND GORGONZOLA TART

At Caffè Museo, this savory country tart is served with an arugula salad for lunch.
Purple plums may be substituted for the figs.

2 pints (3 baskets) fresh figs, stemmed
and halved or 8 plums, pitted and
thinly sliced

2 tablespoons extra-virgin olive oil

Pinch of salt

Pastry Dough (see Basics)

^{1}/2 cup (1 oz/30 g) fresh bread crumbs

1^1/2 cups (8 oz/125 g) crumbled
Gorgonzola cheese or fresh white
goat cheese

2 tablespoons minced fresh thyme

1 egg beaten with 1 tablespoon heavy
cream

■ Preheat the oven to 350°F (180°C). Line a baking sheet with aluminum foil.
In a medium bowl, combine the figs or plums, olive oil, and salt; toss to coat.
■ On a lightly floured surface, roll the dough out to a 12-inch (30-cm) diameter.
Sprinkle the bread crumbs over the dough, leaving a 1^1/2-inch border around the
edge. Sprinkle the Gorgonzola or goat cheese over the bread crumbs. Sprinkle
the thyme over the cheese. Arrange the figs or plums evenly on top. Fold the
edge of the dough over the ingredients, pleating as you go. Brush the crust with
the egg mixture. Bake in the preheated oven for 30 to 40 minutes, or until the
pastry is golden brown. Remove from the oven and transfer the tart to a wire
rack. Let cool before slicing into wedges. *Makes 1 tart; 8 servings*

SEMOLINA GNOCCHI

Recipes for semolina gnocchi can be traced back to Imperial Rome. Serve the gnocchi with sautéed mushrooms or drizzle them with truffle oil—or do both for a wildly extravagant dish.

4 cups (32 fl oz/1 l) milk
1/2 cup (4 oz/125 g) butter
1 1/2 cups (7 1/2 oz/235 g) semolina or
  farina*
1 teaspoon salt
1/2 cup (2 oz/60 g) grated Parmesan
  cheese, plus more for sprinkling
6 egg yolks
4 tablespoons (2 oz/60 g) butter, melted

SAUTÉED MUSHROOMS
2 tablespoons olive oil
1 pound (500 g) assorted mushrooms,
  such as chanterelles, cremini,
  porcini, and stemmed shiitakes,
  sliced
Salt and freshly ground pepper to taste

Truffle oil for serving (optional)

■ Butter a 9-by-13-inch (23-by-33-cm) baking dish. In a large, heavy saucepan, combine the milk and butter. Bring to a simmer over medium heat. When the butter melts, gradually whisk in the semolina or farina and salt. Reduce heat to low and cook, stirring constantly, for 20 to 30 minutes, or until thickened. Remove from heat and let cool slightly. Whisk in the 1/2 cup (2 oz/60 g) Parmesan cheese and the egg yolks. Using a wet spatula, spread the semolina or farina out smoothly in the prepared baking dish. Let cool for about 30 minutes.
■ Preheat the oven to 450°F (230°C). Butter an 8-inch (20-cm) square oven-proof serving dish.
■ With a 1 1/2-inch (4-cm) biscuit cutter or shot glass, cut the semolina or farina into disks. Transfer the disks to a buttered ovenproof serving dish, arranging them in a single layer that overlaps like roof tiles. Brush with melted butter and sprinkle with Parmesan cheese. Bake for 30 minutes, or until lightly golden.
■ To make the mushrooms: In a large frying pan over medium-high heat, heat the olive oil and sauté the mushrooms until liquid is released and then evaporated. Season with salt and pepper. Top the gnocchi with the mushrooms and serve immediately. If desired, drizzle with truffle oil. *Makes 6 servings*

* A coarsely ground durum wheat, imported Italian semolina can be found in specialty foods stores and Italian markets. Farina, a wheat cereal widely available under the brand name Cream of Wheat, may be substituted.

JAMES WEEKS *Two Musicians* 1960

DEEP-DISH APPLE AND RHUBARB CRISP

This recipe also works well with peaches and blackberries, or apples and cranberries.

3/4 cup (2 oz/60 g) rolled oats
$^1/_2$ cup ($2^1/_2$ oz/75 g) all-purpose flour
1 cup (7 oz/220 g) packed brown sugar
$^1/_2$ teaspoon ground cinnamon
$^1/_4$ teaspoon salt
$^1/_2$ cup (4 oz/125 g) unsalted butter,
  melted

4 Granny Smith apples, peeled, cored,
  and cut into bite-sized pieces
4 rhubarb stalks, peeled if stringy, cut
  into slices $^1/_2$ inch (12 mm) thick
2 tablespoons fresh lemon juice
$^1/_2$ cup (4 oz/125 g) sugar

■ Preheat the oven to 425°F (220°C). In a medium bowl, combine the oats, flour, brown sugar, cinnamon, and salt. Stir in the butter until the mixture resembles coarse crumbs.

■ In a large bowl, combine the apples and rhubarb. Stir in the lemon juice and granulated sugar.

■ For individual crisps, fill eight $3^1/_2$-inch (9-cm) ovenproof ramekins or cups with the fruit mixture. Drop spoonfuls of topping over the fruit; the topping does not need to completely cover the fruit. Alternatively, add the fruit mixture to an 8-inch (20-cm) square baking dish and cover with spoonfuls of topping. Bake in the preheated oven for 15 minutes. Reduce the oven temperature to 350°F (180°C) and bake for 45 minutes. Remove from the oven and let cool slightly. Serve warm. *Makes 8 servings*

WAYNE THIEBAUD *Dessert Tray* 1992–1994

SEATTLE ART MUSEUM
SEATTLE, WASHINGTON

The Seattle Art Museum is an important artistic and cultural resource for Seattle and the Pacific northwest. My show [Dale Chihuly: Installations at the Seattle Art Museum, June 1992] was the first one-man show by a contemporary artist in the new downtown museum location. It was a big show, and there was an area that wasn't working. At the last minute I had the glassblowers start making some very simple shapes—they looked like yellow balloons and we made about 500 of them. We did it quickly, in about a ten-day period prior to the opening of the show. I decided they would hang well—it was really kind of a fluke, but it worked. When we put it up it was twelve feet high and must have weighed one thousand pounds. That was the beginning of my Chandelier series. As an artist, I congratulate the Seattle Art Museum on its continuing efforts to provide a place for the nourishing of the human spirit. —Dale Chihuly

T he Seattle Fine Art Society, the parent institution of the Seattle Art Museum (SAM), was founded in 1908. The Society's first public exhibition was a display of 439 Japanese prints on loan from Seattle residents. The Art Society became the Seattle Art Museum in 1931, and two years later the museum opened the doors to its new home in Volunteer Park. When the museum outgrew its original facilities, a new building was designed by Pritzker Prize–winning architect Robert Venturi. Completed in 1991, the building is located in the heart of downtown Seattle. In 1994, most of the museum's extensive holdings in Asian art were relocated to the original facilities in Volunteer Park, now called the Seattle Asian Art Museum. The Seattle Art Museum has matured into a world-class arts institution with a global perspective.

SAM is renowned for its Northwest Coast Native American collection. A group of Native American elders and advisors contributed information about masks, sculpture, textiles, and decorative household objects to ensure that the museum offered a context for the works on display. SAM's holdings of African and Asian art are also significant, and its collection of Japanese art—including ink painting, calligraphy, Buddhist sculpture, metalwork, and folk textiles—is one of the most distinguished outside Japan. The museum's modern art collection focuses on

JAN MIENSE MOLENAER *The Duet* c. 1629

MENU

SAM CAFÉ

■

Salmon-Corn Cakes

Short Ribs Braised in Ale

*Potato and
Celery Root Gratin*

*Gingered
Nectarine-Blueberry Crisp*

American and European paintings, sculpture, drawings, prints, and photographs, and works by contemporary Pacific Northwest artists are highlighted.

SAM offers special activities for children and their adult companions during monthly Free First Saturdays, and throughout the year there are daylong family festivals that celebrate art and music with performances, storytelling, and hands-on art projects for children. Local teachers find exciting classroom resources on-line at the museum website, and they can attend professional development workshops and seminars that explore cultural and artistic traditions from around the world.

Every Thursday evening SAM opens for Thursday After Hours and presents well-known jazz artists and contemporary music that ranges from Celtic to Brazilian to African pop. The galleries and the Museum Café are open, and poetry readings, lectures, and films are often offered as well. The Museum Café is located in a light-filled mezzanine and is a favorite for lunch with Seattle residents and tourists alike. The menu's fresh and flavorful salads, soups, entrées, and desserts are often inspired by current exhibitions, and many are Northwest regional dishes, such as SAM Salmon Cakes (page 172) and Salade Niçoise Northwest. The following recipes were created by chef Betsy Davidson.

WINSLOW HOMER *The Salmon Net* c. 1882

SALMON-CORN CAKES

These salmon cakes are one of the most popular lunch dishes at SAM Café, but they also make a great appetizer. Delicious with a glass of chilled Chardonnay.

SALMON-CORN CAKES
2 pounds (1 kg) salmon fillet, pin
  bones and skin removed, finely
  diced (salmon trimmings are fine)
3 green onions, including some green
  parts, thinly sliced
Kernels cut from 2 ears fresh corn
1 teaspoon minced garlic
1 teaspoon Tabasco sauce
$^{1}/_{2}$ teaspoon Worcestershire sauce
1 egg, beaten

$^{1}/_{4}$ cup (1$^{1}/_{2}$ oz/45 g) finely diced red
  bell pepper
$^{1}/_{4}$ cup ($^{1}/_{2}$ oz/15 g) fresh bread crumbs
1 teaspoon salt
Freshly ground pepper to taste

2 tablespoons olive oil
Watercress sprigs for garnish (optional)
Red Pepper Rémoulade (recipe follows)
Tri-Color Slaw (recipe follows)

■ In a large bowl, mix all the salmon-corn cake ingredients together. Mash a little until the mixture just holds together. Shape into $^{1}/_{4}$-cup (2 oz/60 g) patties to make appetizers, or $^{1}/_{3}$-cup (3 oz/90 g) patties to make entrée portions.
■ In a large frying pan over medium-high heat, heat the olive oil until it shimmers. Sauté the cakes for 3 minutes on each side, or until lightly golden. Arrange 2 cakes on each plate. Garnish with watercress sprigs and dollop with the rémoulade. Serve with slaw. *Makes 8 appetizer servings or 6 entrée servings*

TRI-COLOR SLAW

2 large carrots, peeled and shredded

1/2 small red cabbage, cored and
  shredded

1/2 small green cabbage, cored and
  shredded

1/3 cup (3 oz/90 g) sugar

1/2 cup (4 fl oz/125 ml) apple cider
  vinegar

1 1/2 teaspoons caraway seeds

■ In a large glass or ceramic bowl, combine the carrots and cabbage. In a small
bowl, combine the sugar, vinegar, and caraway seeds. Whisk to blend.

■ Pour the dressing over the cabbage mixture and mix well. Let marinate for
4 hours before serving.

RED PEPPER RÉMOULADE

1 tablespoon capers, minced

1 tablespoon finely chopped
  cornichon

1 red bell pepper, roasted, peeled, and
  finely chopped (see Basics)

1 1/2 teaspoons Dijon mustard

1 tablespoon minced fresh flat-leaf
  parsley

1 tablespoon minced fresh dill

1 1/2 teaspoons fresh lemon juice

1/2 cup (4 oz/125 g) mayonnaise

1/2 teaspoon minced garlic

■ In a medium bowl, combine all the ingredients. Stir to blend. *Makes about 1 cup*
(8 fl oz/250 ml)

WATANABE SEITEI *Carps and Waterplants* c. 1900

SHORT RIBS BRAISED IN ALE

Serve this robustly flavored, simple-to-prepare main dish with Potato and Celery Root Gratin (following) or noodles. Ask the butcher to saw the rib slab into thirds across the ribs, not between them.

3 pounds (1.5 kg) lean beef short
   ribs*, cut lengthwise into thirds
2 tablespoons olive oil
Salt and freshly ground pepper to taste
4 carrots, peeled
2 onions, diced
One 12-ounce (375-ml) bottle ale,
   preferably Pike Place Ale

$^1/_2$ cup (4 oz/125 g) tomato paste
2 tablespoons minced garlic
1 bay leaf
2 cups (16 fl oz/500 ml) beef stock
   (see Basics) or canned low-salt beef
   broth

■ Cut between the ribs to make small riblets. In a large Dutch oven or heavy flameproof casserole over medium-high heat, heat the olive oil until it shimmers. In batches, add the ribs, season with salt and pepper, and brown on both sides. Transfer to a plate.

■ Reduce heat to medium and stir in the carrot and onions; sauté until the vegetables are just beginning to brown. Pour in the ale and stir to scrape up any browned bits from the bottom of the pan. Stir in the tomato paste. Add the ribs and cook over medium-high heat to reduce the liquid by half. Stir in the garlic, bay leaf, and stock or broth. Reduce heat to very low, cover, and simmer for about 2 hours, or until the meat is very tender. Skim off any fat. Taste and adjust the seasoning. Remove the bay leaf and serve immediately. *Makes 6 servings*

POTATO AND CELERY ROOT GRATIN

A flavorful side dish to serve with meats, poultry, and game.

2 tablespoons butter

1 onion, diced

3/4 cup (6 fl oz/180 ml) heavy cream
or half-and-half

1¹/₂ cups (6 oz/185 g) grated Parmesan
cheese

Salt and freshly ground pepper to taste

1 tablespoon minced fresh rosemary

¹/₂ celery root, peeled, halved, and cut
into thin half-moons

3 russet potatoes, peeled and thinly
sliced

¹/₂ cup (2 oz/60 g) fresh bread crumbs

■ Preheat the oven to 400°F (200°C). Lightly oil an 8-inch (20-cm) square baking dish.

■ In a large frying pan, melt the butter over medium heat and sauté the onion for 5 minutes, or until golden. Remove from heat and set aside.

■ In a large bowl, combine the cream or half-and-half, ³/₄ cup (3 oz/90 g) of the Parmesan, the salt, pepper, and rosemary. Add the celery root, potatoes, and sautéed onion. Toss to mix well. Transfer the mixture to the prepared baking dish and spread evenly. Cover with aluminum foil and bake in the preheated oven for 45 minutes. Remove the foil and sprinkle with the bread crumbs and remaining ³/₄ cup (3 oz/90 g) Parmesan cheese. Bake for 15 minutes, or until golden brown; serve immediately. *Makes 4 to 6 servings*

DALE CHIHULY *Goblet* 1971–1972

GINGERED NECTARINE-BLUEBERRY CRISP

Serve this delectable crisp in summer, when nectarines and blueberries are at the height of their season.

TOPPING

1 cup (5 oz/155 g) all-purpose flour

1 cup (8 pz/250 g) sugar

1/2 cup (4 oz/125 g) chilled butter, cut
   into cubes

1/2 teaspoon ground ginger

FILLING

6 nectarines, peeled, pitted, and sliced

2 cups (8 oz/250 g) fresh or thawed
   frozen blueberries

1/4 cup (1 1/2 oz/45 g) all-purpose flour

3/4 cup (6 oz/185 g) sugar

1 teaspoon ground cinnamon

2 tablespoons minced candied ginger

■ Preheat the oven to 350°F (180°C). Butter eight 1-cup (8 fl oz/250 ml) ramekins or an 8-cup (64-fl-oz/2-l) baking dish.

■ In a food processor, combine all the topping ingredients and process until the mixture resembles coarse crumbs.

■ In a large bowl, combine all the filling ingredients. Toss to mix. Spoon into the prepared ramekins or baking dish. Cover evenly with the topping, pressing lightly to compact. Bake in the preheated oven for 25 minutes, or until the fruit is soft and the topping is browned. Remove from the oven and let cool slightly or completely. Serve warm or at room temperature. *Makes 4 to 6 servings*

FRANZ MARC *Die grossen blauen Pferde (The Large Blue Horses)* 1911

WALKER ART CENTER
MINNEAPOLIS, MINNESOTA

They gave me the chance to do what an artist strives to do: to create a new work without knowing what the result will be: to take the risk of starting from zero . . . the Walker has always had a legacy of fearlessness, intellectual rigor, and integrity . . . I hardly have words to express my gratitude. —Meredith Monk, Composer, singer, filmmaker, choreographer, director

From paintings and sculptures to videos, installations, dance, and music, the Walker Art Center showcases innovative contemporary work. Originally a small-scale regional institution, the Walker has evolved into a vital center for twentieth- and twenty-first century art.

An internationally renowned permanent collection serves as the centerpiece for the many cultural offerings found at the Walker. More than nine thousand paintings, sculptures, videos, prints, drawings, photographs, artists' books, and installations showcase the major artists and artistic movements of the twentieth century. The Walker often begins to acquire work by young artists early in their careers and continues to collect pieces as the artists mature. In this way, the center has acquired in-depth collections of work by Claes Oldenburg, Roy Lichtenstein, Jasper Johns, and others. New exhibits from the museum's permanent collections are displayed every two years. In addition to lending artwork to major institutions around the world, the Walker brings important exhibitions from other museums to the Minneapolis area.

The eleven-acre Minneapolis Sculpture Garden, one of the largest urban sculpture parks in the United States, is located directly across the street from the Walker. The famous *Spoonbridge and Cherry* fountain sculpture by Claes Oldenburg and Coosje van Bruggen (page 191) was designed for the garden. Seasonal plantings, live birds, and a huge glass-and-wood sculpture, *Standing Glass Fish,* by California architect Frank Gehry (page 183), fill the garden's conservatory.

Over one hundred performance events are commissioned and presented each year at the Walker. Artists from around the world, from masters to emerging performers, are featured in the largest museum-based program in the country. Also

notable is the Film/Video Department, which is widely recognized for its innovative program of retrospectives and screenings of new work. The Two Rivers Native Film Showcase and the Women with Vision series are two of the varied film programs sponsored or cosponsored by the Walker Art Center.

Lectures, films, classes, performances, and family programs develop connections between the art of our time and the Minneapolis community. The Walker's Teen Programs serve as a national model for alternative ways to teach young people about modern art, and Walker on Wheels, a mobile art lab, takes the museum to schools, parks, and festivals.

The Walker's restaurant is located on the eighth floor in a thoroughly modern setting with spectacular views of downtown Minneapolis. Gallery 8 Restaurant offers fresh American cooking with international influences. The café is a family-owned business that was founded in 1979 and is now managed by the original owner's daughter. Chefs Paul Gregory and Bill Williams and pastry chef Gary Robertson created the following recipes.

FRANK GEHRY *Standing Glass Fish* 1986

ANTIPASTO TASTING PLATE

Literally, antipasto *means "before the meal," and this selection of eggplant, bell peppers, asparagus, olives, and crostini (see Basics) makes an appetizing starter.*

1/2 small globe eggplant

2 tablespoons olive or canola oil, plus oil for drizzling

2 tablespoons plus 1 cup (8 fl oz/250 ml) balsamic vinegar

1/2 teaspoon minced garlic

Salt and freshly ground pepper to taste

2 red bell peppers, roasted and peeled (see Basics)

16 asparagus, preferably 12 white and 8 green, peeled and cut into 5-inch (13-cm) lengths

1/2 baguette

1/2 garlic clove

1/4 cup (2 oz/60 g) fresh white goat cheese at room temperature

1 tablespoon crushed toasted pistachio nuts (see Basics)

1 large bunch flat-leaf parsley, stemmed

Pinch of salt

3/4 cup 96 fl oz/180 ml) olive oil

1/2 tablespoon pine nuts, toasted (see Basics)

12 mixed Kalamata and oil-cured black olives

1/2 tablespoon capers

■ Preheat the oven to 400°F (200°C). Cut the eggplant crosswise into rounds 1/4 inch (6 mm) thick, then cut into sticks about the size of French fries. In a medium bowl, toss the eggplant with the 2 tablespoons olive or canola oil, the 2 tablespoons vinegar, the garlic, salt, and pepper. Transfer to a baking sheet and spread out in a single layer. Bake in the preheated oven for 5 to 10 minutes, or until soft. Remove from the oven and set aside.

■ Meanwhile, pour the 1 cup (8 fl oz/250 ml) balsamic vinegar into a small nonreactive saucepan and boil over medium heat until reduced to 1/4 cup (2 fl oz/60 ml).

■ In separate pots of salted boiling water, blanch the white and green asparagus for about 4 minutes, or until crisp-tender. Drain and run under cold water; drain again and set aside.

■ Cut 4 thin diagonal rounds from the baguette; rub each round with the garlic clove and drizzle with oil. Bake in the preheated oven for 5 to 10 minutes, or until golden brown. Let cool and spread with the goat cheese. Sprinkle the crostini with the pistachios.

■ In a blender or food processor, combine the parsley and salt. With the machine running, gradually add the 1^1/$_2$ cups (12 fl oz/375 ml) olive oil to make an emulsified sauce. Strain the parsley oil through a fine-mesh sieve.

■ To serve, divide the eggplant among 4 plates and arrange 3 white and 2 green asparagus pieces (tips at 12 o'clock) over the eggplant. Drape a roasted pepper half over the bottom of the asparagus and tuck the pepper under the vegetables, with the tips of the asparagus and some of the eggplant exposed at the top. Sprinkle with pine nuts, olives, and capers. Drizzle the reduced balsamic vinegar and parsley oil around the plates. Lean a goat-cheese crostini against each serving of vegetables and serve. *Makes 4 servings*

SWORDFISH WITH MUSHROOM RAGOUT AND SOFT PARMESAN POLENTA

This dish is also delicious made with sliced roast chicken substituted for the swordfish.

MUSHROOM RAGOUT

2 tablespoons olive oil

1 small onion, diced

1 pound (500 g) mixed mushrooms such as cremini, stemmed shiitakes,
   and oysters

1 cup (8 fl oz/250 ml) dry white wine

1 fennel bulb, trimmed and sliced crosswise

6 artichoke hearts, sliced (see Basics)

1 cup (8 fl oz/250 ml) chicken stock or canned low-salt chicken broth

$^1/_4$ cup (2 oz/60 g) veal demi-glace*

Salt and freshly ground pepper to taste

SOFT PARMESAN POLENTA

4 cups (32 fl oz/1 l) chicken stock (see Basics) or canned low-salt chicken broth

$^3/_4$ cup (5 oz/155 g) polenta

2 tablespoons butter

$^1/_4$ cup (2 oz/60 g) grated Parmesan cheese

Salt and freshly ground pepper to taste

2 tablespoons olive oil

4 swordfish fillets

Salt and freshly ground pepper to taste

1 tablespoon *each* minced fresh flat-leaf parsley and thyme, plus 4 sprigs *each*
   fresh thyme and flat-leaf parsley

(continued)

- To make the ragout: In a large frying pan over medium heat, heat the olive oil and sauté the onion for 4 minutes, or until soft. Increase heat to high, add the mushrooms, and sauté for about 7 minutes, or until the mushrooms release their liquid and the liquid evaporates. Add the wine and stir to scrape up the browned bits from the bottom of the pan. Add the fennel and artichokes, reduce heat to medium, and cook for 10 minutes. Add the stock or broth and simmer for 15 minutes. Season with salt and pepper.
- To make the polenta: In a medium saucepan, bring the stock or broth to a boil over high heat. Whisk in the polenta, reduce heat to low, and simmer, stirring constantly, for 30 minutes. Stir in the butter, Parmesan cheese, salt, and pepper.
- Preheat the oven to 375°F (190°C). In a large ovenproof frying pan over medium heat, heat the olive oil until it shimmers. Season each fish fillet on both sides with salt and pepper and sear for 2 minutes on each side, or until golden. Place the pan in the preheated oven and bake for 10 minutes, or until the fish is opaque throughout.
- Spoon one-fourth of the polenta into the center of each of 4 plates. Ladle the mushroom ragout over and sprinkle with the minced thyme and parsley. Top with a fish fillet. Garnish each serving with a sprig of thyme and parsley and serve immediately. *Makes 4 servings*

* Veal demi-glace is a concentrated syrup of veal stock that adds richness to sauces and soups. It is available from Williams-Sonoma, at (800) 541-2233, but if you don't have it, the ragout tastes delicious without it.

ROBERT MOTHERWELL *Music for J. S. Bach* 1989

CHERRY SPOONBRIDGE SUNDAE

Named for the Spoonbridge and Cherry fountain sculpture by Claes Oldenburg and Coosje van Bruggen, this fabulous sundae consists of a scoop of brownie pudding and vanilla ice cream topped with macerated cherries, a dollop of whipped cream, and a fresh cherry. At Gallery 8, it is served with a spoon-shaped cookie that mimics the shape of the sculpture.

BROWNIE PUDDING

1¹/3 cups (7oz/220 g) all-purpose flour

1 tablespoon baking powder

¹/2 teaspoon salt

1 cup (8 oz/250 g) plus 2 tablespoons
granulated sugar

3¹/2 tablespoons plus 2 teaspoons
unsweetened cocoa powder

³/4 cup (6 fl oz/180 ml) milk

3 tablespoons butter, melted

1¹/2 teaspoons vanilla extract

1 cup (4 oz/125 g) chopped walnuts

1 cup (7 oz/220 g) plus 2 tablespoons
packed brown sugar

1¹/3 cups (11 fl oz/330 ml) hot water

CHERRY SAUCE

1 pound (16 oz/500 g) fresh Bing
cherries, pitted

1¹/2 cups (12 fl oz/375 ml) dry red
wine

Grated zest of 1 lemon

¹/2 cup (4 oz/125 g) sugar

2 tablespoons cornstarch

³/4 teaspoon almond extract

2 pints vanilla ice cream

¹/2 cup (4 fl oz/125 ml) heavy cream,
beaten to soft peaks

6 fresh Bing cherries with stems for
garnish

■ Preheat the oven to 350°F (180°C). Butter an 8-inch (20-cm) square baking dish.

■ To make the brownie pudding: In a large bowl, combine the flour, baking powder, salt, sugar, and 3¹/2 tablespoons of the cocoa. Stir to blend. Stir in the milk, butter, and vanilla and mix until just combined. Stir in the walnuts. Spread in the prepared baking dish.

■ In a medium bowl, combine the brown sugar, the 2 teaspoons cocoa, and the hot water. Whisk to blend and pour over the batter in the dish.

■ Reduce the oven temperature to 325°F (165°C) and bake the brownie pudding for 20 minutes. Reduce the oven temperature to 300°F (150°C) and bake 40 minutes longer. The pudding will be gooey. Remove from the oven and let cool slightly or completely.

■ Meanwhile, make the cherry sauce: In a medium saucepan, combine the cherries, wine, lemon zest, and sugar. Cook for 5 minutes, or until the cherries are soft. Remove from heat. Transfer 2 tablespoons of the cherry juice to a small bowl and let cool. Whisk in the cornstarch. Stir this mixture back into the cherries and bring the sauce to a boil over medium-high heat for a few seconds, or until thickened and clear. Remove from heat and stir in the almond extract.

■ To serve, place 1 scoop brownie pudding in each of 6 bowls. Top with a scoop of vanilla ice cream and spoonfuls of cherry sauce. Add a dollop of whipped cream and garnish with a cherry. *Makes 6 servings*

CLAES OLDENBURG AND COOSJE VAN BRUGGEN *Spoonbridge and Cherry* 1988

BASICS

ARTICHOKE HEARTS

Trim off the stems of the artichokes and any dark green leaves. With a large, sharp knife, cut off the top 1 inch of the artichokes. Place the artichokes, stem side down, into a large nonreactive pot in which they fit snugly. Add water to cover the artichokes and bring the water to a boil. Reduce heat and simmer, uncovered, for 30 to 45 minutes, or until a leaf can be easily removed and the artichoke bottoms are tender when pierced with a knife. Using a slotted spoon, transfer the artichokes to a plate and set them aside, upside down, to cool. Using a sharp knife, remove the leaves. Using a teaspoon, dig out the chokes.

BROWN BUTTER

In a frying pan, melt the butter over medium heat. Cook until browned, shaking the pan constantly so the solids do not rest on the bottom of the pan and burn. Immediately pour into a bowl.

COCONUT MACAROONS

2 egg whites
$^2/_3$ cup (5 oz/155 g) sugar
2 tablespoons flour
Pinch of salt
1 teaspoon vanilla extract
$1^1/_2$ cups (6 oz/185 g) sweetened shredded coconut

Preheat the oven to 325°F (165°C). Line baking sheets with parchment paper.

In a medium bowl, beat the egg whites until soft peaks form. Gradually beat in the sugar until stiff, glossy peaks form. Beat in the flour, salt, and vanilla. Stir in the coconut. Drop mounds of the mixture from a tablespoon onto the prepared baking sheet and bake in the preheated oven for 15 minutes, or until lightly browned. Remove from the oven and let the cookies cool on the sheets. Store in an airtight container. *Makes about 24 cookies*

CRÈME ANGLAISE

This light custard sauce can be used as a topping or be pooled under desserts.

4 egg yolks
$^1/_2$ cup (4 oz/125 g) sugar
$1^1/_3$ cups (11 fl oz/330 ml) milk
2 teaspoons vanilla extract

In a medium saucepan, whisk the egg yolks until blended. Gradually whisk in the sugar and continue whisking for 2 to 3 minutes, or until the mixture is pale and thick. In a small saucepan, heat the milk over medium-low heat until bubbles form around the edges of the pan. Gradually whisk the hot milk into the egg mixture. Return to the pan and cook, stirring constantly with a wooden spoon over medium heat, until the sauce thickens enough to coat the spoon. Do not let the custard boil or the yolks will scramble. Remove from heat and stir in the vanilla. Let cool completely. Store, covered, in the refrigerator for up to 3 days. *Makes about 1 cup (8 fl oz/250 ml)*

CROSTINI

1 baguette, cut into $^1/_2$-inch-thick (12-mm) slices
Extra-virgin olive oil for brushing

Preheat the broiler. Arrange the bread slices in a single layer on a baking sheet and place under the broiler for 2 to 3 minutes, or until lightly toasted. Remove from heat and brush with olive oil on both sides. Return to the broiler and toast on the other side. Serve immediately, or let cool completely. Store in an airtight container for up to 1 week.

PASTRY DOUGH

1 cup (5 oz/155 g) all-purpose flour
7 tablespoons (3^1/$_2$ oz/105 g) cold unsalted butter, cut into pieces
^{1}/$_8$ teaspoon salt
3 tablespoons cold water

In a food processor, combine the flour, butter, and salt and process until the mixture resembles coarse crumbs, about 15 seconds. With the machine running, add the water and process until the dough begins to form a ball, about 20 seconds. On a lightly floured surface, flatten the dough into a disk, cover with plastic wrap, and refrigerate for at least 45 minutes.

On a lightly floured surface, roll the dough out to an 11-inch (28 cm) circle for a 9-inch (23-cm) tart pan or a 12-inch (30-cm) round for a 10-inch (25-cm) pan. Fit into the pan and trim the edges. Prick the pastry with a fork and refrigerate for 20 minutes. Preheat the oven to 375°F (190°C). Line the shell with aluminum foil and fill with dried beans or pastry weights.

PARTIALLY BAKED PASTRY SHELL: Bake in the preheated oven for 20 minutes, or until lightly colored. Remove the beans or weights and aluminum foil. Prick the bottom of the pastry with a fork and continue baking for 10 minutes, or until lightly browned all over.

FULLY BAKED PASTRY SHELL: Bake in the preheated oven for 20 minutes, or until lightly colored. Remove the beans or weights and aluminum foil. Prick the pastry with a fork and continue baking for 20 minutes, or until golden brown. Let cool for at least 10 minutes before filling.

Makes one 9- or 10-inch (23- or 25-cm) pastry shell

ROASTING PEPPERS AND CHILIES

Roast whole peppers or chilies on a grill, directly over the flame on a gas stove, or in a cast-iron frying pan over medium-high heat, turning to char on all sides. Or, cut large peppers or chilies into fourths, seed, press to flatten, and char under a preheated broiler. Using tongs, transfer the peppers or chilies to a paper or plastic bag, close it, and let the peppers or chilies cool for 10 to 15 minutes. Remove from the bag, peel off the skin with your fingers or a small, sharp knife, and core and seed the peppers or chilies if charred whole.

ROASTED GARLIC

A sweet yet mildly pungent spread.

1 whole garlic bulb   Extra-virgin olive oil for brushing

Preheat the oven to 350°F (180°C). Using a sharp knife, trim the roots from the garlic head and cut off the top of the bulb, exposing the individual garlic cloves. Brush or rub the garlic bulb with olive oil and wrap in aluminum foil. Seal tightly and place in the preheated oven for 1 hour, or until soft. Remove from the oven and let cool. Unwrap the garlic and squeeze out the pulp.

TO PEEL AND SEGMENT CITRUS FRUIT

Cut off the top and bottom of an orange, grapefruit, or lemon down to the flesh, then stand the fruit upright and cut off the peel in sections down to the flesh. Working over a bowl to catch the juice, hold the fruit in one hand and cut between the membranes. Rotate the fruit and let the sections fall into the bowl. Pick out any seeds.

CUTTING AND SLICING A MANGO

Hold the mango upright on a cutting board with a narrow side facing you. Using a large knife, cut off one "face" (the flat side) of the fruit. Repeat on the other flat side. To cut into slices, score the flesh of each half into crosswise slices and push each half inside out. Cut each slice away from the skin.

Sugar Syrup

1 cup (8 oz/250 g) sugar $^{1}/_{4}$ cup (2 fl oz/60 ml) water

In a medium saucepan over medium heat, stir the sugar and water until the liquid is perfectly clear. Remove from heat and let cool completely. To store, cover and refrigerate. Makes about 1 cup (8 fl oz/250 ml)

Toasting Nuts

Spread the nuts on a baking sheet and bake in a preheated 350°F (180°C) oven, stirring once or twice, for 5 to 10 minutes, or until fragrant and very lightly browned.

Toasting Seeds

Heat a small, dry frying pan over medium-high heat. Add the seeds and cook, stirring, for 3 to 4 minutes, or just until fragrant. Immediately empty the seeds into a bowl to cool.

Tortilla Chips

8 tortillas

Preheat the oven to 300°F (150° C). Lightly coat a baking sheet with canola oil. Cut each tortilla into 6 even wedges. Arrange the tortilla pieces on the prepared pan and bake in the preheated oven for about 7 minutes,. Turn the chips over and bake for about 7 minutes longer, or until crisp. Watch carefully, as the chips can burn very quickly. *Makes 48 chips*

STOCKS

BEEF STOCK

4 pounds (2 kg) meaty beef shanks,
  sliced
2 tablespoons olive oil
1 onion, chopped
1 carrot, peeled and chopped
1 celery stalk, chopped
1 bay leaf

3 fresh flat-leaf parsley sprigs
6 black peppercorns
1/2 cup (4 fl oz/125 ml) dry white wine
3 quarts (3 l) water
1/2 cup (4 fl oz/125 ml) tomato purée
Salt and freshly ground black pepper
  to taste

Preheat the oven to 400°F (200°C). In a roasting pan, toss the bones with the olive oil to coat them evenly. Roast for 30 to 40 minutes, or until well browned, turning occasionally. Transfer to a stockpot.

Pour the fat out of the roasting pan. Place the pan over medium heat, add the wine, and stir to scrape up the browned bits from the bottom of the pan. Pour this liquid into the stockpot. Add all the remaining ingredients. Bring to a boil and skim off any foam that rises to the top. Simmer slowly, uncovered, for 3 to 4 hours, or until the stock is well flavored.

Strain through a sieve into a bowl and let cool completely. Cover and refrigerate overnight. Remove and discard the congealed fat on the surface. Store in the refrigerator for up to 3 days. To keep longer, bring to a boil every 3 days or freeze for up to 3 months. *Makes about 4 cups (32 fl oz/1 l)*

CHICKEN STOCK

2 onions, coarsely chopped

Bouquet garni: 4 parsley sprigs,
    4 peppercorns, 1 thyme sprig, and
    1 bay leaf, tied in a cheesecloth
    square

4 pounds (2 kg) chicken bones and
    bony parts such as backs, necks,
    and wings

2 carrots, peeled and chopped

3 celery stalks, chopped

5 garlic cloves

In a stockpot, combine all the ingredients and add water to cover by 2 inches (5 cm). Bring to a boil and skim off any foam that forms on the surface. Reduce heat to low and simmer, uncovered, for $1^1/2$ to 2 hours, or until the stock is well flavored. Strain through a fine-mesh sieve into a clean container. Let cool completely, cover, and refrigerate overnight. Remove and discard the congealed fat on the surface. Store in the refrigerator for up to 3 days. To keep longer, bring to a boil every 3 days, or freeze for up to 3 months. *Makes about $2^1/2$ quarts (2.5 l)*

FISH STOCK

4 pounds (2 kg) heads and bones of
    white-fleshed fish such as sole or
    whiting, cut up

8 cups (64 fl oz/2 l) water

1 carrot, peeled and sliced

2 onions, chopped

1 celery stalk, sliced

Bouquet garni: 6 parsley stems,
    4 peppercorns, 1 fresh thyme sprig,
    and 1 bay leaf, tied in a cheesecloth
    square

1 cup (8 fl oz/250 ml) dry white wine

In a stockpot, combine the fish heads, bones, and water. Bring to a boil, skimming off the scum that rises to the surface. Reduce heat to low, add all the remaining ingredients, and simmer, uncovered, for 30 minutes. Remove from heat and strain through a sieve into a large saucepan. Bring to a boil and cook to reduce the liquid by about one third. Use now, or let cool completely, cover, and refrigerate for up to 2 days. To keep longer, bring to a boil every 2 days, or freeze for up to 2 months.

CONVERSION CHARTS

WEIGHT MEASUREMENTS

STANDARD U.S.	OUNCES	METRIC
1 ounce	1	30 g
1/4 pound	4	125 g
1/2 pound	8	250 g
1 pound	16	500 g
1 1/2 pounds	24	750 g
2 pounds	32	1 kg
2 1/2 pounds	40	1.25 kg
3 pounds	48	1.5 kg

VOLUME MEASUREMENTS

STANDARD U.S.	FLUID OUNCES	METRIC
1 tablespoon	1/2	15 ml
2 tablespoons	1	30 ml
3 tablespoons	1 1/2	45 ml
1/4 cup (4 tablespoons)	2	60 ml
6 tablespoons	3	90 ml
1/2 cup (8 tablespoons)	4	125 ml
1 cup	8	250 ml
1 pint (2 cups)	16	500 ml
4 cups	32	1 l

OVEN TEMPERATURES

FAHRENHEIT	CELSIUS	GAS MARK
250°	120°	1/2
275°	135°	1
300°	150°	2
325°	165°	3
350°	180°	4
375°	190°	5
400°	200°	6
425°	220°	7

Note: For ease of use, measurements have been rounded off.

CONVERSION FACTORS

OUNCES TO GRAMS: Multiply the ounce figure by 28.3 to get the number of grams.

POUNDS TO GRAMS: Multiply the pound figure by 453.59 to get the number of grams.

POUNDS TO KILOGRAMS: Multiply the pound figure by 0.45 to get the number of kilograms.

OUNCES TO MILLILITERS: Multiply the ounce figure by 30 to get the number of milliliters.

CUPS TO LITERS: Multiply the cup figure by 0.24 to get the number of liters.

FAHRENHEIT TO CELSIUS: Subtract 32 from the Fahrenheit figure, multiply by 5, then divide by 9 to get the Celsius figure.

LIST OF MUSEUMS

THE ART INSTITUTE OF
CHICAGO
111 South Michigan Avenue
Chicago, IL 60603
(312) 443-3600
www.artic.edu
Mon, Wed–Fri 10:30–4:30; Tues
10:30–8; Sat–Sun 10–5.

THE CLEVELAND MUSEUM
OF ART
11150 East Boulevard
Cleveland, OH 44106
(216) 421-7340
www.clevelandart.org
Tues, Thurs, Sat–Sun 10–5;
Wed, Fri 10–9. Closed Mon.

DALLAS MUSEUM OF ART
1717 North Harwood
Dallas, TX 75201
Phone: (214) 922-1200
www.dm-art.org
Tues–Wed, Fri–Sun 11–5;
Thurs 11–9. Closed Mon.

DENVER ART MUSEUM
100 W. 14th Avenue Parkway
Denver, CO 80204
Phone: (720) 865-5000
www.denverartmuseum.org
Tues–Sat 10–5; Wed 10–9;
Sun 12–5. Closed Mon.

THE J. PAUL GETTY MUSEUM
1200 Getty Center Drive
Los Angeles, CA 90049
Phone: (310) 440-7300
www.getty.edu
Tues–Thurs, Sun 10–6;
Fri–Sat 10–9. Closed Mon.

HIGH MUSEUM OF ART
1280 Peachtree Street, N.E.
Atlanta, GA 30309
(404) 733-4444
www.high.org
Tues–Sat 10–5; Sun 12–5.
Closed Mon.

LOS ANGELES COUNTY
MUSEUM OF ART
5905 Wilshire Boulevard
Los Angeles, CA 90036
(323) 857-6000
www.lacma.org
Mon–Tues, Thurs 12–8; Fri 12–9;
Sat–Sun 11–8. Closed Wed.

THE METROPOLITAN MUSEUM
OF ART
1000 Fifth Avenue at 82nd Street
New York, NY 10028
(212) 535-7710
www.metmuseum.org
Tues–Thurs, Sun 9:30–5:30;
Fri–Sat 9:30–9:00. Closed Mon.

THE MUSEUM OF MODERN ART
MoMA's 53rd Street building
is closed for construction May
2002–2005. During this time,
highlights of the museum's
permanent collection and
temporary shows will be
exhibited at MoMA QNS, in
Long Island City, Queens.

MOMA
11 West 53rd Street
New York, NY 10019
(212) 708-9400

MOMA QNS
45-20 33rd Street
Long Island City, NY 11101
(212) 708-9400
www.moma.org
Mon, Thurs, Sat–Sun 10–5; Fri
10–7:45. Closed Tues and Wed.

MUSEUM OF FINE ARTS,
BOSTON
Avenue of the Arts
465 Huntington Avenue
Boston, MA 02115
(617) 267-9300
www.mfa.org
Mon–Tues 10–4:45; Wed–Fri
10–9:45; Sat–Sun 10–5:45.

THE MUSEUM OF FINE ARTS,
HOUSTON
1001 Bissonnet
Houston, TX 77005
(713) 639-7300
www.mfah.org
Tues–Wed 10–5; Thurs 10–9;
Fri–Sat 10–7; Sun 12:15–7.
Closed Mon.

NATIONAL GALLERY OF ART
Sixth Street at Constitution
Avenue, N.W.
Washington, D.C. 20565
(202) 737-4215
www.nga.gov
Mon–Sat 10–5; Sun 11–6.

PHILADELPHIA MUSEUM
OF ART
Benjamin Franklin Parkway at
26th Street
Philadelphia, PA 19103
(215) 763-8100
www.philamuseum.org
Tues–Sun 10–5; Wed, Fri
10–8:45. Closed Mon.

SAN FRANCISCO MUSEUM
OF MODERN ART
151 Third Street
San Francisco, CA 94103
(415) 357-4000
www.sfmoma.org
Mon, Tues 11–6; Thurs 11–9;
Fri–Sun 11–6. Closed Wed.

SEATTLE ART MUSEUM
100 University Street
Seattle, WA 98101
(206) 654-3255
www.seattleartmuseum.org
Tues–Wed, Fri–Sun 10–5;
Thurs 10–9. Closed Mon.

WALKER ART CENTER
Vineland Place
Minneapolis, MN 55403
(612) 375-7577
www.walkerart.org
Tues–Wed, Fri–Sat 10–5; Thurs
10–9; Sun 11–5. Closed Mon.

LIST OF ILLUSTRATIONS

LIST OF ILLUSTRATIONS

p 111 PAUL REVERE II American, 1734–1818
Coffee Pot, c. 1791 Silver. Museum of Fine Arts, Boston.
Bequest of Buckminster Brown, M.D., MFA:95.1359.
p 100 JOHN SINGER SARGENT American, 1856–1925
*Mrs. Fiske Warren (Gretchen Osgood) and Her Daughter
Rachel*, 1903. Oil on canvas, 60"x 40³/₈" (152.4 x 102.6
cm). Museum of Fine Arts, Boston. Gift of Mrs. Rachel
Warren Barton and the Emily L. Ainsley Fund,
MFA:64.693.

MUSEUM OF FINE ARTS, HOUSTON

p 116 CAMILLE COROT French, 1796–1875
Orpheus Leading Eurydice from the Underworld, 1861.
Oil on canvas, 44¹/₄" x 54" (112.3 x 137.1 cm). The
Museum of Fine Arts, Houston. Museum purchase with
funds provided by the Agnes Cullen Arnold Endowment
Fund, 87.190.
p 119 WILLEM CLAESZ HEDA Dutch, 1594–1680
Banquet Piece with Ham, 1656. Oil on canvas, 44" x 60"
(111.7 x 152.3 cm). The Museum of Fine Arts, Houston.
Gift of Mr. and Mrs. Raymond H. Goodrich, 57.56.
p 112 CLAUDE MONET French, 1840–1926
Water Lilies (Nymphéas), 1907. Oil on canvas, 36¹/₄" x
31¹⁵/₁₆" (92.1 x 81.2 cm). The Museum of Fine Arts,
Houston. Gift of Mrs. Harry C. Hanszen, 68.31.
p 115 CRISTOFORO MUNARI Italian, 1667–1720
Still Life with Musical Instruments, c. 1710–1715. Oil on
canvas, 52¹/₂" x 38¹/₄" (133.3 x 97.1 cm). The Museum
of Fine Arts, Houston. The Samuel H. Kress Collection,
61.60.
p 114 *Exterior View of the Audrey Jones Beck Building*
The Museum of Fine Arts, Houston. Photograph
courtesy of Richard Barnes.

MUSEUM OF MODERN ART, NEW YORK

p 122 PABLO PICASSO Spanish, 1881–1973
Three Musicians, Fontainebleau, summer 1921. Oil on
canvas 6' 7" x 7' 3³/₄" (200.7 x 222.9 cm). The Museum
of Modern Art, New York. Mrs. Simon Guggenheim
Fund. © 2002 Estate of Pablo Picasso/Artists Rights
Society (ARS), New York. Photograph © 2002 The
Museum of Modern Art, New York.
p 130 ROBERT RAUSCHENBERG Amercan, b. 1925
Factum II, 1957. Combine painting: oil, ink, pencil,
crayon, paper, fabric, newspaper, printed reproductions,
and painted paper on canvas; 61³/₈" x 35¹/₂" (155.9 x
90.2 cm). The Museum of Modern Art, New York.
Purchase and an anonymous gift and Louise Reinhardt
Smith Bequest (both by exchange). Photograph © 2002
The Museum of Modern Art, New York.
p 125 ANDY WARHOL American, 1928–1987
S & H Green Stamps, 1962. Silkscreen ink on canvas,
71³/₄" x 53³/₄" (182.3 x 136.6 cm). The Museum of
Modern Art, New York. Gift of Philip Johnson. © 2002
Andy Warhol Foundation for the Visual Arts/ARS,
New York. Photograph © 2002 The Museum of Modern
Art, New York.
p 124 *11 West 53rd Street Entrance*. The Museum of
Modern Art, New York. Photograph © 2000 Peter
Harholdt.

NATIONAL GALLERY OF ART

p 143 PIERRE BONNARD French, 1867–1947
Table Set in a Garden, c. 1908. Oil on paper mounted on
canvas, 19¹/₂" x 25¹/₂" (49.5 x 64.7 cm). National
Gallery of Art, Washington. Ailsa Mellon Bruce
Collection, 1970.17.8 (PA). © 2002 Artists Rights
Society (ARS), New York/ADAGP, Paris. Photograph
by Richard Carafelli.
pp 1, 132 MARY CASSATT American, 1844–1926
Afternoon Tea Party, 1890–1891. Drypoint, aquatint, and
gold paint on laid paper, plate: 13¹¹/₁₆" x 10³/₈" (34.77
x 26.35); sheet: 16 3/4" x 12 1/4" (42.5 x 31.1 cm).
National Gallery of Art, Washington. Chester Dale
Collection, 1963.10.256 (PR). Photograph by Dean
Beasom.
p 138 MARC CHAGALL Russian 1887–1985
The Hen with the Golden Eggs, 1927/1930. Etching,
plate: 11⁵/₈" x 9⁷/₁₆" (29.5 x 24 cm); sheet: 14¹⁵/₁₆" x
11¹/₈" (38 x 28.2 cm). National Gallery of Art,
Washington. Rosenwald Collection, 1952.8.173 (PR).
© 2002 Artists Rights Society (ARS), New York/
ADAGP, Paris. Photograph by Dean Beasom.
p 208 HENRI FANTIN-LATOUR French, 1836–1904
Still Life, 1866. Oil on canvas, 24³/₈" x 29¹/₂"
(62 x 74.8 cm). National Gallery of Art, Washington.
Chester Dale Collection, 1963.10.146.
p 2 ORAZIO GENTILESCHI, Florentine 1563–1639
The Lute Player, c. 1612/1620. Oil on canvas, 56¹/₂" x
50³/₄" (143.5 x 129 cm). National Gallery of Art,
Washington. Ailsa Mellon Bruce Fund, 1962.8.1.
p 136 VINCENT VAN GOGH Dutch, 1853–1890
The Olive Orchard, 1889. Oil on canvas, 28³/₄" x 36¹/₄"
(73.0 x 92.1 cm). National Gallery of Art, Washington.
Chester Dale Collection, 1963.10.152 (PA).
p 135 HENRI MATISSE French, 1869–1954
Woman with Amphora and Pomegranates, 1953. Paper
collage on canvas, 96" x 37⁷/₈" (243.6 x 96.3 cm).
National Gallery of Art, Washington. Ailsa Mellon
Bruce Fund, 1973.18.3 (PA). © 2002 Succession H.
Matisse, Paris/Artists Rights Society (ARS), New York.
Photograph by Richard Carafelli.
p 11 CAMILLE PISSARRO French, 1830–1903
The Artist's Garden at Eragny, 1898. Oil on canvas,
28⁷/₈" x 36¹/₄" (73.4 x 92.1 cm). National Gallery of
Art, Washington. Ailsa Mellon Bruce Collection,
1970.17.54 (PA). Photograph by Richard Carafelli.
p 134 *After Dark: View of the East Building (1978)
from the West Building, Fourth Street Entrance*. National
Gallery of Art, Washington. Architect: I. M. Pei &
Partners. Photograph by Dennis Brack/Black Star.

THE PHILADELPHIA MUSEUM OF ART

p 144 GEORGES BRAQUE French, 1882–1963
Violin and Newspaper (Musical Forms), 1912–1913.
Graphite, charcoal, and oil on canvas, 36" x 23¹/₂"
(91.5 x 59.7 cm). Philadelphia Museum of Art. The
Louise and Walter Arensberg Collection, 1950-134-26.
© 2002 Artists Rights Society (ARS) New York/
ADAGP, Paris.

LIST OF ILLUSTRATIONS

p 154 MARCEL DUCHAMP American b. in France, 1887–1968
Chocolate Grinder (No. 1), 1913. Oil on canvas, 24³/₈" x 25³/₈" (61.9 x 64.4 cm). Philadelphia Museum of Art. The Louise and Walter Arensberg Collection, 1950-134-069. © 2002 Artists Rights Society (ARS), New York/ADAGP, Paris/Estate of Marcel Duchamp. Photography by Graydon Wood, 1998.

p 147 THOMAS EAKINS American, 1844–1916
Antiquated Music: Portrait of Sarah Sagehorn Frishmuth, c. 1900. Oil on canvas, 97" x 72¹/₂" (246.4 x 184.1 cm) Philadelphia Museum of Art. Given by Mrs. Thomas Eakins and Miss Mary Adeline Williams, 1929–184-7.

p 153 GEORGIA O'KEEFFE American, 1887–1986
Peach and Glass, 1927. Oil on canvas, 9¹/₈" x 6¹/₁₆" (23.2 x 15.4 cm). Philadelphia Museum of Art. Given by Dr. Herman Lorber, '44-95-4. © 2002 The Georgia O'Keeffe Foundation/Artists Rights Society (ARS), New York.

p 148 *Pennsylvania German Kitchen*, c. 1752. Made in Millbach, Lebanon Country, Pennsylvania. Philadelphia Museum of Art (Museum Views). Gift of Mr. and Mrs. Pierre S. du Pont and Mr. and Mrs. Lammot du Pont. 1926-74-1. Photograph by Graydon Wood, 1989.

p 146 *West Facade of the Philadelphia Museum of Art from the West Bank of the Schuylkill River*. Philadelphia Museum of Art. Photograph by Graydon Wood and Andrew Harkin, 1991.

SAN FRANCISCO MUSEUM OF MODERN ART

p 156 PABLO PICASSO Spanish, 1881–1973
Nature morte "La Cafetière" (Still Life "The Coffee Pot"), 1944. Oil on canvas, 21³/₄" x 17³/₈" (55.25 x 44.13 cm). San Francisco Museum of Modern Art. Bequest of Elise S. Haas, 91.177. © 2002 Estate of Pablo Picasso/Artists Rights Society (ARS), New York.

p 167 WAYNE THIEBAUD American, b. 1920
Dessert Tray, 1992–1994. Oil on board, 19³/₈" x 19¹/₄" (49.21 x 48.9 cm). San Francisco Museum of Modern Art. Collection of Vicki and Kent Logan; fractional and promised gift to the San Francisco Museum of Modern Art, 97.880. © Wayne Thiebaud/licensed by VAGA, New York.

p 165 JAMES WEEKS American, 1922–1998
Two Musicians, 1960. Oil on canvas, 84" x 66" (213.36 x 167.64 cm). San Francisco Museum of Modern Art. Thomas W. Weisel Fund purchase, 84.127.

p 159 EDWARD WESTON American, 1886–1958
Cabbage Leaf, 1931. Gelatin silver print, 7⁹/₁₆" x 9¹/₂" (19.21 x 24.13 cm). San Francisco Museum of Modern Art. Albert M. Bender Collection, Albert M. Bender Bequest Fund Purchase, 62.1169. © Edward Weston.

p 161 *San Francisco Museum of Modern Art*. Photograph by Richard Barnes.

p 158 *San Francisco Museum of Modern Art*. Architect: Mario Botta. Photograph by Richard Barnes.

SEATTLE ART MUSEUM

p 178 DALE CHIHULY American, b. 1941
Goblet, 1971-1972. Glass, 9" x 6" x 7³/₄" (22.9 x 15.2 x 19.7 cm). Seattle Art Museum. Gift of Neil Meitzler, 76.18.

p 171 WINSLOW HOMER American, 1836–1910
The Salmon Net, c. 1882. Charcoal and white chalk on paper; plate: 21¹/₂" x 29¹/₄" (54.6 x 74.3 cm), frame: 32" x 39³/₄" (81.3 x 101 cm). Seattle Art Museum. William Edris Bequest Fund; Margaret E. Fuller Purchase Fund; Richard E. Fuller Aquisition Fund, 74.67.

p 168 JAN MIENSE MOLENAER Dutch, 1609/10–1668
The Duet, c. 1629. Oil on canvas, 25¹/₄" x 19⁷/₈" (64.1 x 50.5 cm). Seattle Art Museum. Gift of the Samuel H. Kress Foundation, 61.162.

p 175 WATANABE SEITEI Japanese, 1851–1918
Carps and Waterplants, c. 1900. Color on silk; overall h. 87³/₄" (222.9 cm), overall w. 23⁷/₈" (60.6 cm); image h. 48¹/₂"(123.2 cm), image w. 15⁹/₁₆" (39.5 cm); diameter roller: 1" (2.54 cm). Seattle Art Museum. Gift of Griffith and Patricia Way, 97.71.2.

WALKER ART CENTER

p 183 FRANK GEHRY American b. in Canada, b. 1929
Standing Glass Fish, 1986. Wood, glass, steel, silicone, Plexiglas, rubber; 264" x 168" x 102" (671 x 427 x 259 cm). Collection Walker Art Center, Minneapolis. Gift of Anne Pierce Rogers in honor of her grandchildren, Anne and Will Rogers, 1986.

p 180 FRANZ MARC German, 1880–1916
Die grossen blauen Pferde (The Large Blue Horses), 1911. Oil on canvas, 41⁵/₈" x 71⁵/₁₆" (105.7 x 181.1 cm). Collection Walker Art Center, Minneapolis. Gift of the T. B. Walker Foundation, Gilbert M. Walker Fund, 1942.

p 189 ROBERT MOTHERWELL American, 1915–1991
Music for J.S. Bach, 1989. Lithograph, chine appliqué on paper; 22¹/₂" x 14¹⁵/₁₆" (57.2 x 37.9 cm). Collection Walker Art Center, Minneapolis. Gift of Margaret and Agnus Wurtele and the Dedalus Foundation, 2000. © 2002 Dedalus Foundation, Inc./Licensed by VAGA, New York, NY.

p 191 CLAES OLDENBURG American b. in Sweden, b. 1929

COOSJE VAN BRUGGEN American b. in Holland, b. 1942
Spoonbridge and Cherry, 1988. Aluminum painted with polyurethane enamel and stainless steel, 29' 6" x 51' 6" x 13' 6" (9 x 15.7 x 4.1 m). Minneapolis Sculpture Garden, Collection Walker Art Center, Minneapolis. Gift of Frederick R. Weisman in honor of his parents, William and Mary Weisman, 1988. Reproduced with permission of the artists.

p 183 *Walker Art Center and the Minneapolis Sculpture Garden*. Photograph courtesy Walker Art Center.

INDEX

ACKNOWLEDGMENTS

I would like to thank the many people who made this volume possible. My deepest gratitude to the musuem café chefs who generously contributed their recipes. Thank you to James N. Wood, Ted Spiegel, Eileen Harakal, and Brad Nugent of The Art Institute of Chicago; Katharine Lee Reid, Julie Limpach, and Denise Hostman of the Cleveland Museum of Art and John Royak of Heck's Catering; John R. Lane, Lisa Moore, Ellen Key, and Jeanne Chvosta of the Dallas Museum of Art; Lewis Sharp, Julie Behrens, David de Parrie, and Rachel McKenzie of the Denver Art Museum; Deborah Gribbon, Libby Rogers, Eve Yeung, Ani Benglian, and Jacklyn Burns of the J. Paul Getty Museum; Michael E. Shapiro, Diana Sauvigné, Amy Simon, and Lauren Shankman of the High Museum of Art and Tony Conway and Christophe Holmes of Legendary Events; Andrea Rich, Jane Conaway, and Shaula Coyl of the Los Angeles County Museum of Art and Pamela Mosher of the Patina Group; Philippe de Montebello, Deborah Winshel, David Mancini, Julie Zeftel, Harold Holzer, and Jennifer Oetting of the Metropolitan Museum of Art; Glenn D. Lowry, Beth Wildstein, Mikki Carpenter, and Gianfranco Sorrentino of the Museum of Modern Art; Malcolm Rogers and Kieran Heffernan of the Museum of Fine Arts Boston; Peter C. Marzio, Lynn Wyatt, Heather Castle, and George Zombakis of the Museum of Fine Arts, Houston and Lee Taylor of Cafe Express; Earl A. Powell III, Deborah Ziska, Judy Metro, Michel Lartigue, and Kristen Fuller of the National Gallery of Art; Anne d'Harnoncourt, Norman Keyes, Laura Coogan, Christine Sullivan, and Jennifer Yeager of the Philadelphia Museum of Art; Libby Garrison, Gordon Drysdale, Tiponya Bliss Miller, and David Sturtevant of the San Francisco Museum of Modern Art; Mimi Gates, Steven Iverson, Erica Lindsay, and Catherine Walworth of the Seattle Art Museum and Ken Clark and Janet Makela of Chihuly Studios; Kathy Halbreich, Karen Gysin, Ann Gale and Tracy Reuter of the Walker Art Center and Linda Coffey.

Affectionate thanks to violinist Nina Bodnar, violinist Henry Gronnier, violist Tom Diener, and cellist Eric Gaenslen of the Rossetti String Quartet. Thank you, Malcolm Addey, assisted by Jesse Nichols, for the excellent recording done at Fantasy Studios in Berkeley, California. Thanks also to Charlotte Schroeder of Colbert Artists Management and Nina Bombardier of Fantasy Studios.

Once again sincere thanks to my friends Paul Moore for his brilliant photographs and Amy Nathan, for her artistic food styling. Thank you to Diane McGauley for her stylish props and also to The Gardener, Berkeley; Trillium Press; Brisbane; The Heritage House Tableware Showroom, San Francisco.

Thanks to Bill Rusconi for the violin that appears on the cover, and to Amy Singer of the Breast Cancer Research Foundation, researcher Linda Ohran Soderquist, and Marilyn Barnett.

Deepest gratitude to my longtime editor Carolyn Miller for her expert advice, editorial guidance, and poetry. Thanks to Jennifer Barry of Jennifer Barry Design for her book and cover design and for her enthusiastic support of this project. Thanks also to Kristen Wurz of Jennifer Barry Design.

Once again, I want to especially thank Sarah Creider, who was central to this entire endeavor. Grateful acknowledgments also go to Sharlene Swacke, Tim Forney, Ned Waring, Erick Villatoro, and Isidro Montesinos of Menus and Music.

And, as always, I am grateful to my daughters, Claire and Caitlin, and to my husband, John, for their inspiration and their love.

HENRI FANTIN-LATOUR *Still Life* 1866 National Gallery of Art